THE  SERIES

P-47 THUNDERBOLT AT WAR

BY CORY GRAFF

ZENITH PRESS

First published in 2007 by Zenith Press, an imprint of Quarto Publishing Group USA Inc., 400 First Avenue North, Suite 400, Minneapolis, MN 55401 USA

Zenith Press titles are also available at discounts in bulk quantity for industrial or sales-promotional use. For details write to Special Sales Manager at Quarto Publishing Group USA Inc., 400 First Avenue North, Suite 400, Minneapolis, MN 55401 USA.

To find out more about our books, join us online at www.zenithpress.com.

Editor: Scott Pearson
Designer: Elly Gosso
Printed in the United States of America

Library of Congress Cataloging-in-Publication Data

Graff, Cory, 1971-
  P-47 Thunderbolt at war / By Cory Graff.
    p. cm.
  ISBN: 978-0-7603-2948-1 (softbound)
  1. Thunderbolt (Fighter planes) I. Title.
UG1242.F5G66 2007
623.74'64—dc22
                    2007017813

About the author:

Cory Graff is the Assistant Curator for Military Collections at The Museum of Flight in Seattle, Washington. In his free time, he works on aviation-related history projects including exhibits and books. He has had articles published in *Air & Space Smithsonian Magazine* and The Museum of Flight's *Aloft* magazine. Graff is the author of two previous books, *Shot to Hell: The Stories and Photos of Ravaged WWII Warbirds* and *Strike and Return: American Air Power and the Fight for Iwo Jima*. He lives in Seattle.

On the cover:
Main: P-47B Thunderbolts of the 56th Pursuit Group patrol over Long Island, New York, in early 1942. The pilot in plane No. 1 is Hubert "Hub" Zemke. He would become an ace and one of America's top fighter commanders, leading the 56th into battle in the skies over Europe. *Stan Piet*

Inset: Sporting the white cowl bands and tail stripes applied to American fighters in the European Theater early in the war, this early-model P-47D was part of the 78th Fighter Group at Duxford. Pilot Lt. Alwin Juchheim would be an ace by war's end. *National Archives*

On the frontispiece: Capt. Fred "Chris" Christensen Jr. of the 56th Fighter Group after he shot down six enemy aircraft on July 7, 1944. Flying his Thunderbolt, *Miss Fire*, he caught a group of Junkers Ju 52 cargo planes preparing to land at a Luftwaffe airfield. *Stan Piet*

On the title pages: Lt. Paul Martin in Hawaii in 1944 next to a 15th Fighter Group Thunderbolt. The plane, *Stinger V*, was flown regularly by future ace Robert "Todd" Moore. *7th Fighter Command Association*

On the back cover: This razorback P-47D Thunderbolt, *Betty*, was a grizzled vet of the 353rd Fighter Group when photographed in the months after D-Day at Raydon, in Suffolk, England. *Stan Piet*

CONTENTS

ACKNOWLEDGMENTS

A book like this cannot be created by a single person. I'd like to thank all of those who helped me with art, translations, suggestions, and information: P. J. Muller, Katherine Williams, Shawn Chamberlain, Tyler Staal, Kelcey Rushing, Key Donn, Joshua Stoff, William Federico, Edward Young, Justin Hotard, Shauna Simon, and Steve Ellis. Those who graciously assisted me in acquiring the images for this volume were Walter Höllhumer, Mark Stevens, Brett Stolle, Alan Renga, Norm Taylor, the late Pete Bowers, Christopher Wright, Katherine Huit, Bill Mohn, and Holly Reed. And thanks to Stan Piet, who years ago collected an amazing assortment of color P-47 shots, many of which are seen in this book. Special thanks to retired colonel and P-47 ace Steve Pisanos, who agreed to be interviewed for this volume. His memoir, *The Flying Greek*, will be released soon. Also, thanks to Steve Gansen and Scott Pearson of Zenith Press, who helped make this book a reality, and copyeditor Tom Kailbourn.

INTRODUCTION

Pilots who flew the Republic P-47 Thunderbolt in combat are often haunted by feelings of anonymity. As one man wrote to his local aviation museum, "I was a P-47 pilot and flew a tour in Europe. I become very disturbed when I see the [North American] P-51 Mustang get all the credit for the victory in Europe. The P-47 shot down more enemy aircraft and did more damage on the ground than any other fighter. In some books you don't even see the P-47 mentioned. In magazines that tout models, you see many replicas but never the P-47. People don't think it a pretty aircraft, but they have not had the opportunity of seeing one in full flight."

I couldn't agree more, except I'd have to say that the Thunderbolt was never very pretty. It was an ugly brute. And one of the most wondrous and fearsome devices man has ever fashioned. The huge fighter earned its reputation through actions, not its looks.

More than fifteen thousand Thunderbolts, often lovingly called "Jugs" by flyers, were built—the most of any American fighter in history. They served in nearly every combat theater during World War II. The Thunderbolt was the biggest, heaviest single-engine fighter of the war, weighing more than a Ford Trimotor passenger plane.

Naysayers said the plane was too massive to fight it out with smaller German and Japanese machines, but seventeen of America's twenty-one top-scoring fighter aces flew the Jug. The supercharged fighter could cruise more than seven miles above the earth and was amazingly powerful and fast. When a Thunderbolt dived from high above, Axis flyers found escape almost impossible. They were forced to fight or turn tail amidst a storm of lead.

The P-47 hefted eight dependable .50-caliber machine guns into the skies, when most other fighters carried six or less. As Republic's media department said, the Thunderbolt had "firepower to shatter the enemy with a single burst."

The airplane could take it too. Pilots coaxed their beloved Thunderbolts home after hitting trees and high-tension wires. Others left horrified crew chiefs counting dozens, sometimes hundreds, of holes in the Jug's battered skin after a particularly hairy mission. Pilots called the plane a "Flying Bulldozer," "Bucket of Bolts," or "The Iron Monster." They said you could fly through a brick wall and live. It turns out they were right.

This often-overlooked predator of the skies could rip apart enemy planes, lug a ton of bombs, ravage ground forces, and, at the end of the day, hit a telephone pole and keep flying. Does it really matter that the airplane wasn't pretty?

The Republic YP-43 Lancer, first flown in March 1940, during a test flight for the army. Note the pair of .30-caliber guns in the nose and the single .50-caliber machine gun in each wing. *Stan Piet*

De Seversky entered the SEV-3, in its landplane configuration, into the army's competition for a trainer aircraft. To fit the requirements, designers revised the cockpit and equipped the plane with dual flight controls and military radio equipment. *The Museum of Flight, Bowers collection*

CHAPTER ONE

BLOODLINES: ORIGINS OF THE P-47

The story of one of the greatest American fighter planes of World War II began on the other side of the globe from the United States, in a different time, before the start of the Great War. Strangely, it was an exiled, crippled Russian combat hero who assembled the company and skilled team that would create the renowned Thunderbolt.

THE MAKING OF "THE MAJOR"

Alexander's father *owned* an airplane. At a time when hardly anyone in the world had ever even seen a flying machine, the aristocratic de Seversky family had one of the first aircraft in all of Russia. Born in the city of Tbilisi in 1894, Alexander Nikolaivitch Prokofiev de Seversky learned how to fly early in life because of his family's wealth and his father's keen interest in all types of mechanical things.

In military school from the age of ten, young de Seversky graduated from the Russian Imperial Naval Academy in 1914. He was serving as a lieutenant on a destroyer in the Baltic Sea when World War I began. After the numbingly cold winter of 1915, de Seversky's rare skill as an experienced flyer enabled him to transfer to Russia's small but rapidly growing corps of aviators.

After attending the Military School of Aeronautics at Sevastopol, Crimea (modern-day Ukraine), de Seversky was again sent to the Baltic Sea, this time as a naval aviator. He was assigned to a squadron of two-man bombers based on the island of Saaremaa in the Gulf of Riga (Saaremaa is now part of the Republic of Estonia). In the summer of 1915, the group of Russian flyers went to war, launching an attack on a flotilla of German destroyers steaming through the area. During their bombing run on the vessels, a wall of gunfire wracked de Seversky's aircraft. Struggling to get back over land, de Seversky lost control of his plane; it smashed into the sea, the remaining bombs on board exploding. The crash and tremendous blast killed the observer assigned to de Seversky and terribly injured his right leg. Doctors amputated below the knee, effectively ending de Seversky's combat career.

After de Seversky recovered from his wounds and had been fitted with a wooden leg, he fought to be reassigned to frontline status. Frustrated with his superiors' views that his artificial leg would diminish his flying skill in combat, the stubborn young man set out to prove them wrong.

Young Alexander de Seversky in the pilot's seat of a rickety Russian biplane bomber. Because his father was a flyer, de Seversky had grown up around aircraft, earning him a spot in the WWI-era Czarist air force. This photo appeared in de Seversky's book, *Victory Through Air Power. Author's collection*

During an aerial exhibition attended by many high-ranking Russian navy officers, the one-legged pilot made an unauthorized flight. De Seversky wrung the plane out—performing loops, rolls, and stunts—trying to show those in attendance that he was a highly skilled flyer, despite his injury. The young man was promptly arrested for his actions.

It was Czar Nicholas II who pardoned de Seversky and returned him to combat duty in the summer of 1916. The gamble paid off. When transferred to pursuit aircraft, de Seversky downed his first enemy aircraft just three days later. In fifty-seven sorties, the one-legged flyer reportedly claimed thirteen aircraft (other sources give the more conservative number of six) and became Russia's leading World War I naval ace.

His story of overcoming a terrible injury, bucking the system, and becoming a highly successful and deco-rated combat ace seemed almost like fiction; de Seversky became a celebrity in Russian military and political circles. One tale told about him may be apocryphal: While visiting a hospital, de Seversky met another man who had recently lost his leg in battle. "The loss of a leg is no great calamity," he reportedly told the injured man. "If you get hit on a wooden leg, it doesn't hurt a bit. Try it." The patient obliged, giving de Seversky a firm whack with his walking stick. "You see," de Seversky said, "if you hit an ordinary man like that, he'd be in bed for five days." De Seversky limped from the room and collapsed in terrible pain. The injured man had whacked the war hero's good leg.

In 1917 he was selected as part of the Russian Naval Aviation Mission sent to the United States to study aircraft design and manufacturing. By the time de Seversky and the other officers had reached America in early 1918, Vladimir Lenin and the Bolsheviks had seized control of the Russian government. De Seversky realized it would be dangerous for him to return to Russia. He and many of the other naval airmen sought to stay in the United States. De Seversky offered his services as an aeronautical engineer and test pilot to the United States' War Department. He was involved in the Curtiss Aeroplane Company's attempts to create an American version of the famous S.E.5 British fighter before the war ended in November 1918.

In the years after the war, de Seversky applied for 364 patents, including those involving air-to-air refueling and a new type of bombsight which he developed with the Sperry Gyroscope Company of Brooklyn, New York. In 1921 he acted as an advisor to Gen. "Billy" Mitchell during his famous bombing demonstrations upon battleships in Chesapeake Bay. It was the gyroscope bombsight that changed Alexander de Seversky's life. When the United States government purchased the rights to the patent in 1923, de Seversky received fifty thousand dollars—a lot of money at the time. He used the capital to start his own business, Seversky Aero Corporation of New York, New York.

He acclimated to life in the United States quickly, marrying a New York socialite and attaining the rank of major in the U.S. Army Air Corps Reserve. He became a naturalized citizen in 1927.

SEVERSKY AERO CORPORATION

Rather than manufacture aircraft, Seversky Aero Corporation produced aircraft parts, instruments, and "aero equipment." Most notable were alternate types of landing gear, which included fitting one Curtiss Jenny training aircraft with a combination roller-and-ski system. Some advertisements can be found in which de Seversky's name is deliberately misspelled as "Severski," to emphasize the *ski* angle. Also as part of the business, "the Major," as de Seversky was known to almost everyone who worked for him, ran a consulting enterprise.

The Seversky Aero Corporation, however, was short-lived. The stock market crash in October 1929 put the company in bankruptcy.

SEVERSKY AIRCRAFT CORPORATION AND ALEXANDER KARTVELI

De Seversky was too stubborn to quit. With backing from investors at a most dubious time in America's financial history, the Major established Seversky Aircraft in early 1931. The idea was to create advanced, all-metal aircraft in their entirety. De Seversky would act as president, designer, and chief test pilot. The Major looked to Russia to find the intellectual know-how he would need to construct his sophisticated airplanes. He hired engineers Michael Gregor and Alexander Kartveli.

Fellow Russian Alexander Kartveli was born in the same town as de Seversky and was also unable to return when the Russian Revolution changed his homeland forever. Kartveli stayed with the Seversky company even after its namesake had departed, designing the famed P-47 Thunderbolt. *Cradle of Aviation Museum*

Kartveli, the man who would eventually lead the P-47 program, was, like de Seversky, born in Tbilisi and served in the Russian military during World War I. He was sent to Paris in 1918 to study military tactics. Like de Seversky, he was compelled to stay in his host country as Czarist Russia succumbed to revolution.

In France, Kartveli made ends meet by taking an odd combination of jobs—circus trapeze artist and math teacher—while he studied to attain degrees in aeronautical and electrical engineering. Later, he worked at various French aviation companies before setting out to America to pursue better opportunities.

While working briefly at nearby New Jersey and New York aviation firms, fellow countrymen de Seversky and Kartveli soon met. As the Major established his new aircraft company, he hired Kartveli to assist chief engineer Gregor with the design of the first Seversky aircraft.

THE SEV-3 AMPHIBIAN

Downtown New York City was no place to build planes, so de Seversky reached an agreement with the Edo Aircraft Corporation of College Point, Long Island, to house the construction of the initial aircraft. Edo was a logical choice: the company was located on the water and was the country's leading manufacturer of metal floats. The Major's first creation was an amphibian, perhaps influenced by the efforts of his first company to develop landing-equipment technology for use beyond the realm of prepared runways. The aircraft, called the Sport Amphibian, would be equipped with floats to land on water or snow or with wheels to land on runways. Both the main wheels (recessed in the bottoms of the floats) and the entire floats could be raised and lowered hydraulically to provide for either landing configuration or for aerodynamic efficiency in cruising flight.

Because it would carry three flyers, the first Seversky airplane was dubbed the SEV-3. The airframe was highly advanced, featuring many design characteristics and the basic layout that would be the basis for the company's airplanes through the P-47 fighter and beyond. A low-wing monoplane with Alclad aluminum skin, the beefy airplane sported beautiful elliptical wings and a streamlined dorsal canopy.

After the SEV-3's first flight in June 1933, the Major achieved a new international speed record of 179.7 miles per hour on October 9. Soon after, the plane underwent the first of a series of changes. Among these were new

The big, fast Sport Amphibian was de Seversky's first aircraft, designated the SEV-3 because it was designed to carry three people. Equipped with Edo floats, the aircraft could land on water or land. Note the *Sever Sky* logo painted on the side of the fuselage. *The Museum of Flight, Bowers collection*

landing gear, floats, structural adjustments, and various engines.

It soon became clear that the Sport Amphibian was too expensive and complex for all but the wealthiest sportsman of the time. The average civilian flyer could afford little more than a small, rickety biplane. De Seversky and his crew decided to pursue the military. Competing for an army basic trainer contract in 1935, the SEV-3, flying without its floats, was a hit at Wright Field, at Dayton, Ohio. The SEV-3 proved superior to the entry from North American Aviation, and the Seversky Company was awarded a contract to build thirty aircraft, designated the BT-8 trainer.

The SEV-3 was a hot ship. Wright Field evaluators recognized the Seversky machine compared favorably to the Boeing P-26 "Peashooter," still one of the army's frontline fighters of the era. With only a slightly slower top speed, the SEV-3 was getting the job done while

pulling one thousand extra pounds, all while the plane's engine delivered significantly less horsepower.

With the right engine, it seemed, the BT-8 trainer would be equal to all but the best pursuit airplanes. But in a backhanded way, the army assured that the BT-8 trainer would stay a trainer plane, and not a good one at that. With added military equipment, the trainer was eight hundred pounds heavier than the demonstrator and carried a four hundred-horsepower Pratt & Whitney R-985 radial engine, thus limiting its ability. While de Seversky

The Seversky BT-8 was the army's first all-metal, enclosed cockpit monoplane trainer aircraft. While it was modern in appearance, the plane was also underpowered and had narrow-track landing gear, which made it prone to ground-loop accidents—not exactly stellar traits for a basic-training plane. *The Museum of Flight*

recommended an engine of 500 horsepower or more, army regulations required training planes to have 400 or less. Those who flew the BT-8s feared them as chronically underpowered and, therefore, quite dangerous to inexperienced flyers—not a good trait for a trainer!

THE P-35

The remarkable fact that de Seversky's first plane was one of the best American aircraft flying inspired him to seek more improvements, refinements, and horsepower. Could his wonderful machine be reborn once more as a fighter plane?

Soon, de Seversky installed a 715-horsepower Wright R-1820 engine in the nose of the SEV-3. The aircraft set a new amphibian speed record of 230 miles per hour. But the first and only SEV-3 would only go so far; a new airframe was already taking shape in Seversky's plant in Farmingdale, Long Island.

With de Seversky on the road selling aircraft, the company moved to the airport at Farmingdale to make room to build BT-8s. The Major was not pleased with the move "to the country," and as a result Michael Gregor left the company. De Seversky moved Kartveli into the top design spot.

The new airplane was designated the SEV-2XP, a two-place experimental pursuit. Similar in size to the SEV-3, the new plane looked as if it was part of the growing Seversky family, with fixed landing gear enclosed in spats and elliptical wings. Besides the pilot, the aircraft had a gunner's station in the aft part of the

Inexplicably, de Seversky's pursuit plane entry had a second station equipped with a rear-mounted machine gun. An accident damaged the plane, fortunately allowing the Seversky team to convert their SEV-2XP into the SEV-1XP, with only one seat. *The Museum of Flight, Bowers collection*

"The Major" pilots his SEV-1XP fighter over New York City. The image is typical de Seversky, with Manhattan's sprawling skyline in the background and none other than Alexander himself at the controls. *The Museum of Flight, Bowers collection*

cockpit—a strange configuration for a pursuit plane.

On the way to Wright Field for evaluation, the plane was involved in an accident. While it was undergoing repairs, the army (as well as the Curtiss pursuit entry) had to wait. This "lucky accident" enabled the Major to make vital changes to his design. In the shop, the SEV-2XP underwent a massive transformation. The rear station was faired over, making the plane a true one-man machine. The fighter now had a huge "baggage compartment" where the gunner had been. The single-place airframe received a new designation to reflect the change—SEV-1XP. Furthermore, de Seversky installed a newly designed retractable landing gear system.

In Dayton, Seversky, Curtiss, Consolidated, and Vought worked out the kinks in their respective aircraft. For Seversky, it entailed the painful process of replacing the problematic Wright R-1670 with a Pratt & Whitney R-1830, rated at 850 horsepower.

None of the teams were able to get their airplane flying reliably (let alone flying fast) for any length of time. Frustrated officials were forced to cancel the competition and try again the following spring, 1936. That year,

the problems continued, particularly with the engines. After the competition, Seversky won a contract for seventy-seven aircraft, designated P-35s.

Looking elsewhere in the aviation world in 1936 must have been painful for U.S. Army officials. In the uneasy climate of Europe, Germany and Great Britain were designing fighter planes that were vastly superior in technology and performance to the new Seversky P-35. The Messerschmitt Bf-109, Supermarine Spitfire, and Hawker Hurricane—planes that would dominate the early air battles of World War II—were close to becoming operational fighting aircraft. Compared to the P-35's struggle to reach more than 260 miles per hour, early Bf-109s could attain nearly 300. The prototype Hurricane flew to 320, and the first Spitfire, an astonishing 360 miles per hour.

With little else to choose from, the men at Wright Field committed to the Seversky P-35. Slightly later, as war in Europe became imminent, the army hedged its bets by taking a second look at the Curtiss entry, the runner-up to the Seversky plane in the competition. This airplane would later become the Curtiss P-36 Hawk.

The 1st Pursuit Group, based at Selfridge Field near

On April 30, 1937, de Seversky flies an early version of the P-35 for the cameras. Note the large, fully enclosed pods that shield the main gear wheels and tires from the slipstream. Pilots said that when the gear was extended, the rear of the fairings acted as air scoops. Production versions of the P-35 had partly covered wheels, partially alleviating the problem. *The Museum of Flight, Taylor collection*

Parked outside a Selfridge Field hangar, the P-35s of the 27th Pursuit Squadron, 1st Pursuit Group, await another flight. The squadron is the oldest in United States' service, established during World War I. The 27th's planes carried the "Fighting Eagle" insignia on their sides. *National Archives*

Detroit, Michigan, received the first P-35s. From 1938 to 1940, the group also flew P-36s, alternating between the Seversky pursuits in the morning and the Curtiss craft in the afternoon. During this time, the flyers and mechanics in the group argued over which plane was better.

By the time Japan attacked Pearl Harbor, Hawaii, on December 7, 1941, the P-35's days were numbered. Only around fifty remained in active service, and they were to be phased out soon afterward. Many were used for training mechanics at aviation schools. By the end of hostilities, only one airframe remained. It can be seen today, fully restored, at the National Museum of the United States Air Force in Dayton, Ohio.

THE BATTLE OF THE SUPERCHARGERS

At Seversky, no one was sitting on their laurels after the 1936 fighter competition. Building warplanes for the army and foreign nations was like hitting a fast-moving target in these uncertain times.

After Seversky produced the last P-35, the Major and Kartveli convinced the army to return the plane to the company for further modifications. De Seversky was keenly aware of the trend toward fighters that could perform at higher altitudes, and amazingly, the army seemed to be half listening to his pleas.

However, even with a P-35 airframe available for experimentation, de Seversky kept an ace up his sleeve: a second airframe of his own, which received similar modifications concurrently. The military dubbed the improved P-35 the XP-41. Seversky named its own project the AP-4. Both aircraft eliminated the P-35's pesky rearward folding, partially retractable landing gear. Each of the newer planes had a differing system that produced the same results: the main gear folded inward, toward the fuselage, and the strut and wheel were stowed completely within the wing.

The other significant change was the addition of a supercharger on the XP-41 and its companion, the AP-4.

The improved P-35 was designated the AP-9 by the company and the XP-41 by the army. It featured fully retractable gear and a supercharger. Famed aviatrix Jackie Cochran flew this aircraft to a new speed record of 332 miles per hour in April 1940. *The Museum of Flight, Williams collection*

The supercharger allowed an aircraft engine to perform at higher altitudes, where the air is much thinner than it is at sea level. The device works by collecting air, condensing it, and feeding it to the engine. A supercharger is neither small nor light. De Seversky and Kartveli studied various options for locating it within the fuselage. The nose was a logical choice because it offered certain advantages, most notably a short air ducting system between the supercharger and the engine. However, the location proved to pull the plane's center of gravity forward and reduced visibility for the pilot.

After long deliberation, they settled on placing the device in the plane's belly. That extra large compartment in the rear, a holdover from the SEV-2XP days, suddenly became a blessing. The location of this critical piece of equipment stayed the same during the design and development of the future P-47 Thunderbolt.

Both the XP-41 and the AP-4 took on General Electric superchargers, located in the fuselage just behind the trailing edge of the wings. One difference separated the two; the XP-41's system was a supercharger, mechanically geared to the engine. The AP-4's system was a turbo

supercharger, which ran off of the engine's exhaust gas. The gases propelled a turbine, which in turn powered the compressor.

The army's make-or-break line was razor thin. In 1939, though the XP-41 showed a small advantage over the P-35 and P-36 by flying at around 320 miles per hour, the improvement was insufficient, and the project died. The Major's AP-4 performed at around 350 miles per hour. The army awarded a contract to Seversky for thirteen service evaluation models, designated YP-43s.

REPUBLIC

More than a year later, when the planes were delivered to the army, they were built by the newly renamed Republic Aviation Corporation. The cost of building the pair of supercharged machines had put the Seversky Aircraft Corporation far into debt. Experimentation with advanced aircraft, the board of directors believed, was terrible business without big orders.

The Major argued that only by moving forward, quickly, could the company succeed. Only through risky steps could the corporation be positioned for great suc-

"The Major" with a bottle of Coca-Cola in the cockpit of the first P-35. Critics argued that de Seversky was a better showman than businessman. Seversky Aircraft Corporation's board of directors certainly thought so, voting him out of his own company. *The Museum of Flight, Bowers collection*

cess. And as the world slowly slipped toward what appeared to be massive global conflict, great success for the company could only be a few months and a few orders away.

While he was in England trying to sell warplanes, the board voted de Seversky out of the presidency. The eight-letter name *Republic* was chosen for the newly organized company because it had the same number of letters as *Seversky*, which made changing the signs all that much easier. Wallace Kellett became president, and Alex Kartveli remained vice-president and chief engineer. The Major was crushed.

THE LANCER AND ROCKET

A 1,200-horsepower Pratt & Whitney R-1830 radial powered the Republic YP-43 Lancer. It carried a pair of .50-caliber machine guns in the wings and two .30-calibers in the nose cowling. There were few changes from the original AP-4. The new plane sported a slightly taller tail wheel, allowing a bit more visibility over the nose. It also

A pilot and his Republic P-43 Lancer are featured in a Curtiss propeller ad in 1941. Later, many P-47 Thunderbolts were also equipped with Curtiss Electric props. *The Museum of Flight, Hatfield collection*

had a lower-profile cockpit enclosure—a design that would carry over to the famous P-47 Thunderbolt. In these last few years before the United States became embroiled in war, the early Lancers lacked self-sealing fuel tanks and armor protection for the pilot.

Nervously looking toward air battles taking place in Europe, the army and Republic's leaders knew that they needed more speed, power, and performance to have a chance against Nazi fighters. The result was an improved version of the Lancer, designated the P-44 Rocket.

The order to build eighty P-44s came well before a P-43 had rolled out of the Republic factory. First incarnations of the plane, nicknamed Rockets, were meant to carry a 1,400-horsepower Pratt & Whitney R-2180. Republic's later design work allowed for an even bigger engine, the Pratt & Whitney R-2800 radial. This engine promised 2,000 horsepower, enough to propel the plane at over four hundred miles per hour. These planes were dubbed P-44 Warriors.

By the time the first YP-43 Lancer was delivered in September 1940, the army had seemingly bought into the idea of the more powerful P-44 Rocket/Warrior: they ordered 827 of them! However, the army was not satisfied. The planes slugging it out in Europe were pointy-nosed, liquid-cooled machines with heavy armor, armament, and self-sealing fuel tanks.

The army began to have second thoughts about buying in on a huge gaggle of Republic P-44 Rockets/Warriors. "Showtime" was just around the corner it seemed, and another performer waited in the wings.

The first version of the Thunderbolt, the XP-47, looked nothing like the famous fighter that would later take shape. In fact, this large-scale mockup at Republic looked unlike any company aircraft designed before or after. The liquid-cooled engine required by the army made the overall appearance of the aircraft more like the Bell P-39 or Curtiss P-40. *Cradle of Aviation Museum*

The fighter plane that never was. This Republic Aviation Corporation artist's concept shows what the XP-44 Rocket would have looked like if it had been completed. It certainly looks the part of a Republic fighter—similar in many ways to the less powerful P-43 Lancer. *Cradle of Aviation Museum*

THE FIRST THUNDERBOLT

Except in designation, the first version of the Thunderbolt was an unrecognizable shadow of what the classic machine would become. It began life as a small gnat of a fighter, equipped with two .50-caliber guns. The plane was to be powered by an Allison V-1710 liquid-cooled engine, similar to those flying in the Lockheed P-38, Bell P-39, and Curtiss P-40 fighters, and was extremely tiny and lightweight.

The army decided it was too small and unequipped for the possible battles ahead. Though undesirable for mass production, the plane had enough intriguing characteristics for the army to ask for an only slightly larger and heavier version equipped with four guns and bomb racks. The army ordered this version in November 1939 under the designation of XP-47.

Actually, there were two planes forthcoming. The XP-47 was on a fast track—built without radio, armament, and other military equipment for a quick initiation of flight tests. This machine was to be completed in nine months. Another aircraft, the XP-47A, would be fully combat equipped for later delivery.

THE TURNING POINT

The army requested senior Republic officials meet with them in Dayton to discuss upcoming fighter requirements and the current contracts for the P-44 and XP-47. Kartveli and others boarded the night train for the ride from New York to Ohio.

The conversations must have left them spinning. Again, closely watching the developments in the skies over Europe, the army said the XP-47 lightweight fighter was a dead end—cancelled. And the army also cast aside the more than eight hundred P-44s, with big engines and projected great performance. The army instead wanted a fighter aircraft with the following:

Super performance: at least four hundred miles per hour at twenty-five thousand feet
Heavy armament: at least six .50-caliber guns, and eight would be even better
Great protection: armor plate for the pilot and self-sealing fuel tanks
Long range: a minimum of 315 gallons of fuel.

If it wasn't for the army's insistence on getting a "better" fighter, the United States might have gone to war with these basic fighter models, as seen in a brochure advertising Curtiss Electric propellers (top to bottom): the Lockheed YP-38 Lightning, the Bell P-39 Airacobra, the Curtiss P-40 Kittyhawk/Warhawk, and the YP-43 Lancer. *Edward Young*

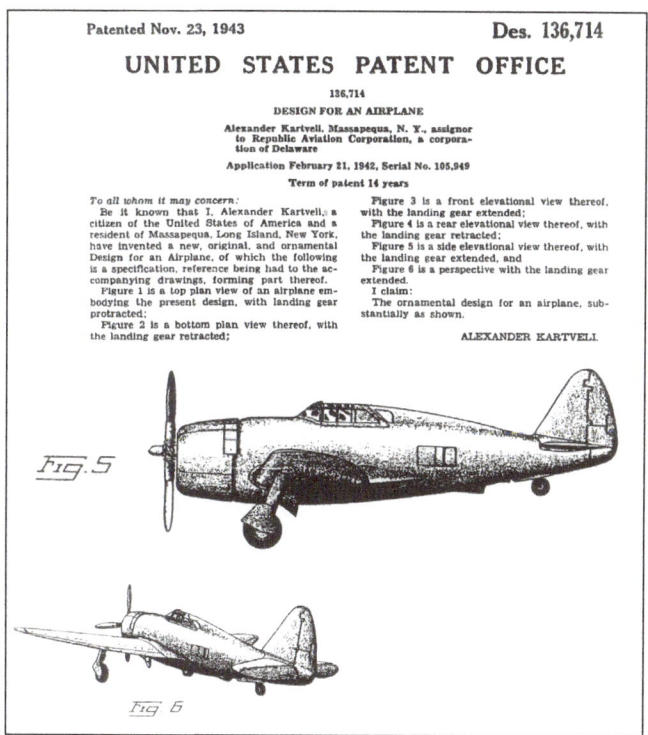

A 1942 patent document submitted by Kartveli and Republic claims rights to the "ornamental design" of the new fighter. Some would say that the look of the big-bellied machine was nothing to be too worried about. What the "Jug" lacked in looks, it more than made up for in fighting performance. *P-47 Fighter Pilot's Association*

This unfortunate landing accident took place in Louisiana in 1942. The strange crash gives one a unique view of the P-43 Lancer's supercharger, nestled in the aft belly of the stricken fighter. *The Museum of Flight, Taylor collection*

The ride home must have been pure misery. Everyone knew the P-43 and XP-47, even heavily modified, revised, stretched, and souped-up, could never touch the requirements. Kartveli figured even his beloved P-44 Warrior, with its amazing R-2800 engine, was just too small to carry the fuel and guns required. They would have to start over yet again.

LANCERS TO WAR

While the army was expecting nothing short of a miracle, they had a considerate side too. With Republic frantically working to devise a new fighter design, the army would keep the factories open building P-43 Lancers. Though outdated and small, the P-43s had uses and even a few advocates.

Claire Chennault's American Volunteer Group (AVG), the Flying Tigers, delivered some export-model P-43s to China. Soon to be famous for their shark-mouthed Curtiss P-40 fighters, some of the AVG pilots reportedly lobbied to keep a few of the Republic planes. They argued that the P-43 had better high-altitude performance, and its air-cooled engine was not as vulnerable to battle damage as the liquid-cooled Curtiss fighter. For the pilots' safety, Chennault denied their requests; the Lancer had no armor and no self-sealing fuel tanks. They were given to the Chinese Air Force, who flew them in combat against the Japanese. The outmoded planes had a dismal record versus more sophisticated Japanese fighters and their skilled pilots.

The U. S. retained some P-43s as training aircraft. Others were stripped down and fitted with cameras in their large rear compartments for use in photo reconnaissance missions. The Royal Australian Air Force received six of these photo aircraft on loan.

U.S. Army Air Forces mechanics perform an engine change on a P-43 Lancer. The somewhat out-dated fighter's Pratt & Whitney R-1830 radial engine was always in demand for Douglas C-47 cargo aircraft. *National Archives*

Two factors contributed to the P-43's demise all over the globe. First, of course, the plane was outdated, even compared to early versions of the P-39 Airacobra and P-40 Tomahawk fighters. And second, the "semi-worthless" Lancer had an engine that was a valuable commodity—compatible with those installed in the venerable Douglas C-47 cargo plane. Many a Lancer was robbed of its power plant to keep a workhorse "Gooney Bird" on the flight line, ferrying cargo and troops.

Colonel Robert L. Scott in his classic book, *God is My Co-Pilot*, wrote about two Chinese P-43A Lancers that had been left at an airfield in Assam, India, in 1943.

He and another bored flyer took the little fighters as their own. He wrote, "...their fuel tanks had developed leaks, and when you added to that the fact that the turbo was underneath the rear of the fuselage, the greatest fire hazard in the world was born."

Scott and his pal did their best to fix them up, stopping the leaks, taking them around the pattern on short flights, and testing their guns by blasting crocodiles in a nearby river. Mount Everest was just three hundred miles away. It was too much to resist. One day, with the turbo supercharger moaning, Scott flew his P-43 two miles above the summit.

The soot-streaked ports aft of the engine compartment were the Thunderbolt's exhaust dumps, which functioned when the hot gases were not required to operate the turbo supercharger. When flying high, the exhaust was directed aft and then pushed overboard, forward of the tail wheel. *The Museum of Flight, Bowers collection*

This cutaway illustration made by Republic artists shows a "skinless" P-47D with a bubble canopy. The image gives an idea of the complexity of the Thunderbolt. The fighter was exceptionally big, but under its web of ribs and stringers, it was packed with equipment for flying and fighting. *The Museum of Flight, Taylor collection*

CHAPTER TWO

BUILDING THE MONSTER: CONSTRUCTION OF THE P-47

Kartveli and his team began work on the new version of the P-47 fighter on their trip back to the East Coast. According to lore, they began the basic layout of the plane on an envelope as the train rumbled along through the night. That may be true, but of course, the entire design and construction of the monster fighter would take much longer.

Looking back, it's amazing to think that the army's hopes (perhaps the nation's hopes) rode on the backs of the designers of an "up-and-down" airplane company that had built a relative handful of airplanes in its short existence. And the army's requirements were extremely advanced—perhaps unrealistic.

THE DOUBLE WASP

Quickly, a "miracle plane" came together on Republic's drawing boards: what *Life* magazine called "just about the most important pursuit ship being built today in the U.S." To provide the needed power for the much larger fighter, Republic designers replaced the XP-47's Allison with Pratt & Whitney's R-2800 Double Wasp air-cooled engine. It was a massive, two-row, eighteen-cylinder radial with a displacement of 2,804 cubic inches. Its cylinder bore was 5.75 inches, and its stroke was 6 inches. The R-2800 was equipped for turbo supercharging, and later versions furnished water injection and ran at 2,250 to 2,800 revolutions per minute. The early versions were touted to turn out 2,000 horsepower, but a shade over 1,600 or 1,700 was more realistically the service output at high altitudes at this early stage.

Not only would the Double Wasp rise to fame for its use in the P-47 Thunderbolt, other designers would employ the engine type too. Nearby on Long Island, perhaps partly inspired by Republic's success, Grumman would use the power plant for the F6F Hellcat. And in Stratford, Connecticut, Vought had already shoehorned the R-2800 into the long nose of the F4U Corsair. In late 1940, the XF4U-1 exceeded four hundred miles per hour on a test flight. Both the Corsair and Hellcat naval fighter planes would dominate the skies over the Pacific in the latter stages of the war. The Double Wasp was also used in the twin-engine Martin B-26 Marauder medium bomber and the Douglas A-26 Invader attack bomber.

More than 125,000 Double Wasps were made, the last

With the cowling off for cleaning, the Thunderbolt's powerful Pratt & Whitney R-2800 radial engine can be seen. The Double Wasp also powered the World War II–era Grumman F6F Hellcat and the Vought F4U Corsair navy fighters. This is an early C-model P-47 at a stateside training facility. *Stan Piet*

built in 1960. During the war, Ford, Nash, Chevrolet, Buick, Continental, and Jacobs all built the engine under license along with Pratt & Whitney.

The R-2800 first ran in 1937 and was first used in an aircraft in 1939. Republic's own experience with the engine went back to mid-1940, when it was chosen for the most powerful version of the P-44, the Warrior. Though no flyable version of the plane was created, a detailed mockup of the fighter used a real R-2800.

Besides providing sufficient horsepower, the 2,360-pound engine proved to be dependable, even when it had sustained terrible damage. In battle, Thunderbolt pilots returned home with entire cylinders blasted away or with the engine block ruptured and a large portion of the plane's oil sprayed over the fuselage.

The pilot's manual for the P-47 listed the engine in the section covering pilot protection. The Double Wasp's bulk and size (more than fifty-two inches in diameter) helped protect the pilot when attacked from the front.

The engine employed simple cooling by air. The propeller and forward motion passed air into the cowling surrounding the engine, where it moved over the Double Wasp's baffled and finned cylinders. The air exited the cowling by way of cowl flaps on the upper rear of the cowling. The pilot could manually operate these flaps,

from fully closed to fully open or anywhere in between.

TURBO SUPERCHARGER AND DUCTING

Designing the P-47 from the inside out, Kartveli and his staff began the process of creating the new fighter with the engine in the nose and the two-stage supercharger, which was to be located in the plane's belly. The physical layout was similar to what the army had seen in the P-43 Lancer design. In between was a lot of real estate: twenty-two feet from the propeller hub to the turbo. The complex system of ducts created to move air from nose to tail and back was designed for maximum efficiency. Only then did the Republic team settle on the P-47's hefty, barrel-chested fuselage, built to surround the multitude of pipes.

Hot, energized air used to power the turbo supercharger was taken from the engine exhaust. Dual half-circular pipes on either side of the engine collected the exhaust gases from each cylinder and routed them aft. Just forward of the plane's firewall, both passages had a waste pipe, branching off the main pipe. Valves, operated by a crank and mechanical rod drive, controlled by the supercharger regulator, could dump the gases overboard through these waste pipes if required.

Should the gases be needed for the turbo, the waste

pipe valves were closed and the gases continued aft down the main pipes, shrouded in stainless steel and asbestos covering to contain the engine exhaust heat. The pair of pipes converged at the turbo supercharger, driving a turbine wheel, which compressed cooler air that had been routed to the aft fuselage in another, separate air duct. The exhaust gases were then expelled via the flight hood, located under the rear of the fuselage, forward of the tail wheel.

A second, larger air duct began at the fighter's nose, under the circular engine within the oval-shaped nose cowling. This duct ran down the lower center of the

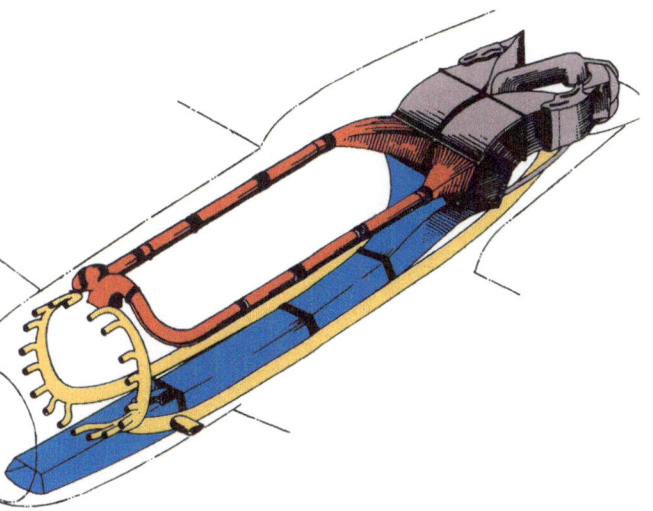

The Thunderbolt's supercharging system was quite complex. In most basic terms, exhaust gases (yellow) powered the supercharger as air (blue) from the lower scoop provided cool, pressurized oxygen. This air (red) traveled forward on either side of the cockpit, into the carburetor. *Cradle of Aviation Museum*

fuselage, splitting into two passages aft of the wings. Air in the lower of the two passages was led through a filter to the upper part of the turbo supercharger, where it was compressed.

As the cool air was compressed and charged, it heated up. The other part of the split duct carried uncharged cool air to lower the charged air's temperature, by means of a box-like intercooler located in the center of the aft fuselage. Operating as an air-to-air heat exchanger, the intercooler transferred the heat

from the charged air, on its way back to the engine, to the air moving in from the upper fork in the duct. The hot air was then dumped overboard through the intercooler exit doors located on each side of the aft fuselage. A pair of ducts routed the compressed and newly cooled air to the R-2800's carburetor, providing clean, cool, compressed air to the Double Wasp at all operational altitudes.

Like the engine, the duct system proved to be tough in combat. Holes blasted into the tubes by enemy fire commonly had no catastrophic effect on the Thunderbolt's overall performance. Pilots who "bellied" P-47s into the ground—crash landing with the landing gear up—found the ductwork acted as a buffer, protecting the flyer's legs. Mechanics liked it too, because the area protected more vital, harder to repair systems farther up in the fuselage from real damage in a gear-up crash.

The supercharging system consisted of two units: One (with an 11.5-inch impeller) received power from the engine mechanically and was defined as a supercharger. The second was a type C-1 turbo supercharger, built by the General Electric Company. It kept the engine humming at high altitude—where it was commonly sixty degrees Fahrenheit below freezing, and the thin air carried one-seventh the atmospheric pressure of that at sea level. The plane's exhaust gases powered this unit.

Ultimate control of this complex system of ducts, valves, and settings was the job of the pilot, who simply maintained a manifold pressure setting from the cockpit. His commands were relayed to an oil-operated supercharger regulator located in the nose, just forward of the firewall and conveniently situated under the plane's main oil tank. This unit translated the pilot's manifold pressure command into a combination of mechanical settings for the positions of the various valves, gates, and doors within the air duct system.

WATER INJECTION

Later versions of the P-47 carried engines that were equipped with water-injection systems for a temporary boost of power beyond normal military settings. Water and alcohol were pumped from a 30-gallon tank affixed to the firewall via an electrically driven pump and injected into the fuel and air mixture. Cooling the mixture and engine somewhat, the water and alcohol allowed more mixture into the cylinder, delayed detonation, and actually

Now that's a heck of an air intake! Flight Officer Herbert Hansen Jr. clowns for the camera in the nose of his Jug in Italy. Half of the air coming through this scoop cooled the other portion, which was leaving the supercharger. The latter traveled back to the engine, through the carburetor. *National Archives*

increased pressure on the pistons in the form of steam.

Called war emergency power (WEP), the water injection allowed pilots in extreme situations to gain a burst of speed or climb rapidly. The WEP system boosted the 2,000-horsepower Double Wasp to perhaps 2,300 or more. But the boost was temporary; there was only so much water in the supply tank, and the burst of power came at the expense of the engine's health. Water in the system and the high rpm power setting were extremely stressful on the engine. Typically, five minutes' worth of WEP power boost was all a flyer could hope for at one time, and it came at the risk of the engine "swallowing a

valve" or some other catastrophic failure. Total time for repeated bursts of WEP was no more than fifteen minutes. After that, the water tank was empty.

PROPELLER

Early Thunderbolts carried a Curtiss Electric propeller. The C642S prop, twelve feet two inches in diameter, had four hollow steel blades. A constant-speed model with manual or automatic blade-pitch selection, the prop lacked feathering or reverse-pitch options. The pilot controlled the propeller via an on/off switch on the main switch box on his left side and a three-place toggle for manual and automatic pitch settings. In the center setting, the prop was linked to the throttle and supercharger control for automatic pitch selection. Pulling

This prewar ad for Republic shows what appears to be a hybrid P-43/P-47-type fighter. The plane has the shape of the Thunderbolt, with a P-47's snout, but the two guns protruding from the cowling are similar to the P-43 Lancer. The aircraft also has six more guns in its wings. *The Museum of Flight, Hatfield collection*

the switch aft would decrease rpm by decreasing pitch. Likewise, pushing the switch forward increased the pitch and rpm.

Later models of the P-47 traded in the thin props—called "toothpicks" by the pilots—for longer, thicker-chord "paddle-blade" propellers. Made by Curtiss Electric and Hamilton Standard, the second iteration of the fighter's thrust source was thirteen feet in diameter and with a wider chord. Controls and capabilities of the system remained basically the same, but the plane's performance increased.

Semi-flat, wide cuffs near the hub distinguished the new paddle props. These cuffs helped cool the engine more efficiently. The bigger propeller (combined with the cuffs) gave the P-47 additional acceleration and increased climbing power. Thunderbolt ace Robert S. Johnson delightedly wrote, "The new prop was worth 1,000 horsepower more, and then some." It added spunk to the big machine that, Thunderbolt pilots had to admit, the airplane really needed to keep competitive with lighter, smaller Axis fighters.

ENGINE LUBRICATION

A twenty-eight–gallon tank located in the upper aft part of the engine compartment provided oil. About nineteen gallons were meant for regular use, with the rest being overload. A pendulum in the tank ensured an uninterrupted flow of oil when the fighter briefly flew inverted.

Oil flowed from the tank into the engine. After used and heated, the oil passed through a pair of cylindrical coolers below the engine. Located on either side of the main air intake for the supercharger, the coolers took advantage of the same blast of atmospheric air pushed into the lower cowling by the propeller and forward motion. After cooling, the oil returned to the tank.

In the cockpit, the pilot managed the oil temperature through electrically operated cowl flaps at the exit of the coolers. A toggle switch on the main switch box on the pilot's left side controlled the shutters. A shutter indicator, located just below the left cockpit rail, showed their position. By opening, closing, or varying settings in between, the flyer controlled the volume of air into the coolers and kept the oil at the proper temperature.

FUEL SYSTEM

The P-47's fuel capacity was always an issue. The army wanted 315 gallons. Initially, Republic shoehorned in 298 gallons into the fuselage. The number soon

The paddle prop on this P-47D helped the Thunderbolt match the performance of enemy fighters, even at lower altitudes. The new propellers carried distinctive flat cuffs near the propeller hub. This aircraft, *Kokomo*, was flown by the 2nd Bomb Group as a control aircraft. *Stan Piet*

increased to 305, carried in two tanks. The main tank, an L-shaped affair, held 205 gallons extending from in front of the cockpit to under the cockpit floor. The second, called the auxiliary tank, was aft of the main tank under the rear cockpit floor and held 100 gallons. These self-sealing tanks were baffled to minimize surge.

Under operational conditions, the 305 gallons carried internally allowed one and a half to two hours in the air and about fifty more miles of range than the British Spitfire. Flying from the UK, the P-47 had a radius of up to two hundred miles without external tanks. While escorting American bombers, the P-47's lack of loiter time frustrated B-17 and B-24 crewmen. They recognized that Luftwaffe pilots knew the P-47's range and

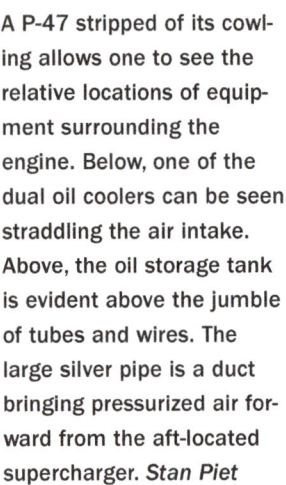

A P-47 stripped of its cowling allows one to see the relative locations of equipment surrounding the engine. Below, one of the dual oil coolers can be seen straddling the air intake. Above, the oil storage tank is evident above the jumble of tubes and wires. The large silver pipe is a duct bringing pressurized air forward from the aft-located supercharger. *Stan Piet*

fuel capacity. The Germans often attacked the bombers as the Thunderbolts turned toward home. P-47 pilots jokingly told their superiors, "The only time we have *too much* gas is when we're on fire."

To stay with the bombers as long as possible, the Thunderbolts began carrying a variety of external fuel tanks, known as "drop tanks" by pilots. The tanks, commonly 75 or 108 gallons, hung from the Thunderbolt's belly or wing pylons. The wing attachments could carry various sizes up to massive 300-gallon tanks. An exhaust vacuum pump pressurized most tanks. The pilot could jettison all external fuel tanks when entering combat.

A P-47 carrying a normal fuel load, including two 108-gallon drop tanks, had more than 500 gallons in total. Thunderbolt pilots flying in Europe thought of it as "200 gallons to fly in, 200 to fly home, and 100 gallons to fight in between."

Later versions of the Thunderbolt, most notably the P-47N built for the Pacific, had improved internal fuel reserves up to 370 gallons in the fuselage and a pair of 93-gallon tanks in the newly designed wing. This gave the long-range N-model 556 gallons carried within the plane's structure and the same capacity as the European Thunderbolts to haul additional fuel in external tanks.

THE P-47'S AIRFRAME

The Wings

The Thunderbolt's wings were three hundred square feet in area, had a root chord of 110 inches, and were nearly forty-one feet from tip to tip (including the fuselage). The aluminum wings were fully cantilevered, with stressed skin and two main spars. The main spars ran span-wise and were attached with hinge fittings to the fuselage with split bushings, pins, and bolts. The main spars were constructed of E-shaped cap strips riveted to webs of varying thickness. Near the fuselage, the webs were .25 of an inch thick. Near the outboard end, they tapered down to a minimum of .032 of an inch. At suitable intervals, the spars held extruded angles which supported frame installations, running parallel to the chord.

Three auxiliary spars supported the aileron, wing flap, and main landing gear. Of those, the one supporting the gear was the thickest, at .091 of an inch thick. The others ranged from .072 to .025 of an inch thick.

Between the spars, flanged Alcad ribs acted as stiffeners. They ranged from .051 to .032 of an inch thick except near the wing root and near the gun bays, where they were a hefty .064 of an inch thick. Additional flanged rib sections formed the leading and trailing edge of the wings.

The wing covering was butt-jointed, flush-riveted stressed aluminum skin reinforced with extruded angle stringers. The skin of the wings was perforated with holes for inspection and maintenance doors and larger openings for the landing gear, machine gun, and ammunition bays. All told, around 16 percent of the wing's skin was panels.

On the top side, reinforced walkways eighteen inches wide near the wing root allowed the pilot to climb in or out of the cockpit on either side. The rest of the wing was not built to hold weight, although photos in this book show many a ground crewman violating that rule.

The ailerons made up about 11.4 percent of the wings and were the Frise type: the nose portion forward

The shape of the Thunderbolt's wings was purely Republic. One could see the distinctive planform in the P-35, P-43, and the much bigger P-47. Republic's company logo showed three of the familiar-shaped fighters climbing through an oval. *National Archives*

of the hinge axis and the lower surface in line with the lower surface of the wing. Similar to the wings, the ailerons had a main spar running span-wise and flanged nose and tail ribs extending fore and aft.

The first P-47s relied on fabric-covered control surfaces, but high-speed dives during testing revealed the fabric could balloon and tear away. Designers switched to aluminum skin covering similar to that of the main wing. The ailerons were controlled by push-pull rods within the wing and control surface structure. The trailing edge of the left aileron held a single trim tab.

Inboard of the ailerons, the fighter's landing flaps constituted 13 percent of the total wing surface. They were National Advisory Committee for Aeronautics slotted type, hydraulically retracted aft and then down, built similarly to the ailerons.

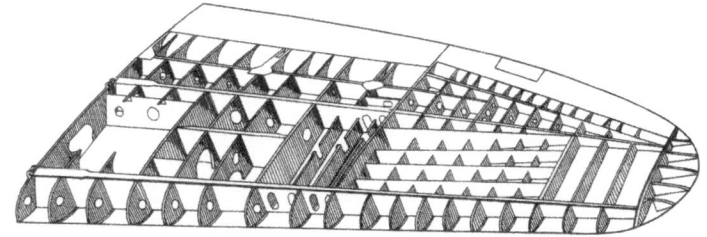

The P-47's wing, designed by Kartveli, was designated Republic S-3. Two main spars extended from the root almost to the tip. Note the break in the ribs for the main wheel and the four holes in the forward spar for the machine gun barrels. *Cradle of Aviation Museum*

During a test flight over Long Island in early 1944, a Republic pilot throttles back and drops the landing gear. The pilot's manual cautioned that the gear should never be lowered at speeds over two hundred miles per hour. The pilot is former Flying Tigers ace Ken Jernstedt, who went on to test aircraft at Republic. *National Archives*

The longer-range P-47N's wings boasted squared-off tips. However, the substantive change was at the opposite end, near the wing root, where 18 inches were added for fuel tanks. Overall, the N-model had a wingspan of slightly over 42.5 feet and a wing area of 322 square feet.

Landing Gear

The main gear units and a tail wheel, all hydraulically operated, supported the heavy P-47. The independent main gear units consisted of a combination air-oil shock strut, extra-high-pressure cast wheels, and rubber tire and inner tube. The system was attached to the main gear spar via a box-like structure made of magnesium plates.

Interestingly, the shock struts were built to telescope. Pinched for space in the wing, the entire unit was shortened by nine inches when retracted, thus leaving more room for the Thunderbolt's eight machine guns and ammunition within the wing structure.

The hearty yet conventional tail wheel fully retracted into a compartment aft of the engine/supercharger exhaust. The tail wheel, when down, could be free-castoring or locked in place by a lever located on the lower right side of the cockpit.

The Tail

The surfaces that made up the tail group, often called the *empennage*, included the horizontal and vertical stabilizers, elevator, and rudder. The makeup of the horizontal and vertical stabilizers was similar, with two main spars with flanged ribs in between and flanged nose ribs extending forward of the leading spar.

The rudder and elevator surfaces consisted of a single spar and ribs at intervals. All three surfaces had trim tabs on the trailing edge. The elevators, built separately but linked when installed on the aircraft, moved together by means of splicing of their torque tubes, in the surface's leading inboard edge.

Besides replacing the fabric-covered rudder and elevators with metal-skinned versions, engineers modified the empennage components after they had torn free during a low-level maneuver. Republic required its subcontractor to "beef up" the tail attachments to the fuselage and general structure.

The Fuselage

The P-47's fuselage consisted of metal transverse bulkheads and longitudinal stringers. The construction was

An exploded view of the vertical tail shows the major components: fin, rudder, and trim tab. *Cradle of Aviation Museum*

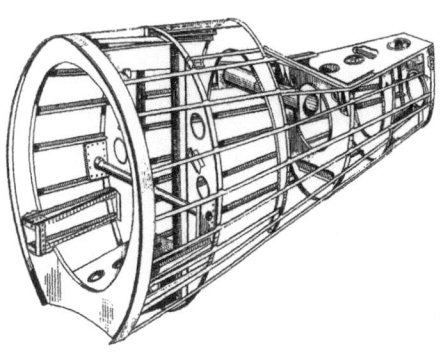

A company drawing shows the stout tail structure, which was attached to the fuselage after the upper and lower halves had been joined. In the factory, the piece was assembled vertically, in a heavy, tubular steel jig. Later, the structure was turned horizontally for skinning. *Cradle of Aviation Museum*

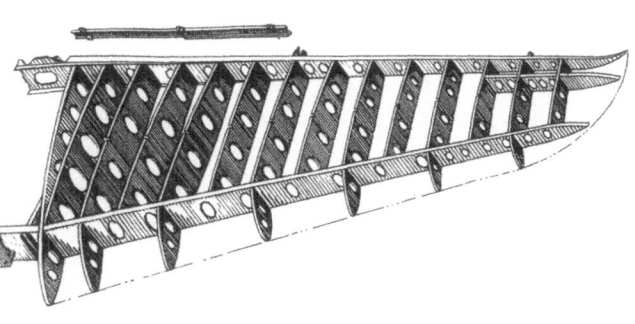

Like many other parts of the Thunderbolt, the horizontal stabilizer was assembled in a jig that could rotate on trunnions, giving assembly workers the best possible position for drilling and riveting the complex metalwork. *Cradle of Aviation Museum*

considered "semi-monocoque," meaning the stressed skin absorbed some of the stresses to which the structure was subjected.

The main fuselage consisted of upper and lower halves. These terminated at bulkhead station number 302 1/2. Aft of that, the tail cone was added to create the entire fuselage structure from firewall to near the end of the tail.

The upper and lower halves were joined at reinforcing angles by bolts and rivets. The forward-most tail cone frame butted against the adjoining aft-most main fuselage frame and the components were likewise bolted and riveted together. Typically, the plane's stressed skin

terminated near each seam, riveted to the structural element running along the break line.

The bulkheads at the forward end of the fuselage helped hold a series of corrugated and flat Alclad metal sheets and pieces of channel section that made up the fighter's firewall. Dual heavier bulkheads were built into the lower half of the main fuselage and served to give strength to the wing attachment components, 3.5-inch wide steel E section steel beams and steel-forged wing hinges. The upper fuselage frame at station number 180 was also bigger and stronger. This frame, located just aft of the cockpit, held the armor plate, protecting the pilot. And near the tail wheel, the frames were likewise beefed up to bear the plane's weight on takeoff and landing.

THE P-47's SYSTEMS

Surface Controls

The pilot manipulated the plane's control surfaces—rudder, ailerons, and elevators—using standard rudder pedals and a control stick. Control rods running aft from the stick transferred motion to the elevator. These ran from under the cockpit floor and went upwards and aft via pivoting swing links attached to the plane's structure. The aft-most rod attached to a control horn inboard of the elevator torque tube.

Aileron controls ran from the stick via rods attached to bell cranks at the sides of the fuselage. They were in turn attached to long push-pull rods extending into the

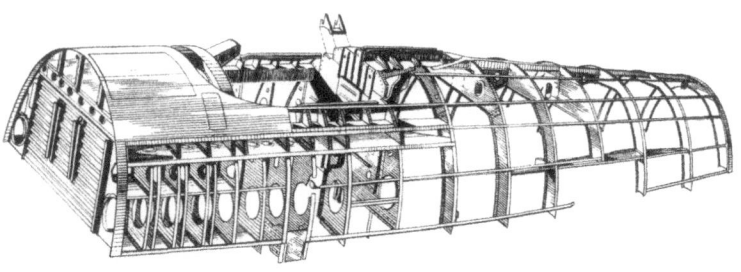
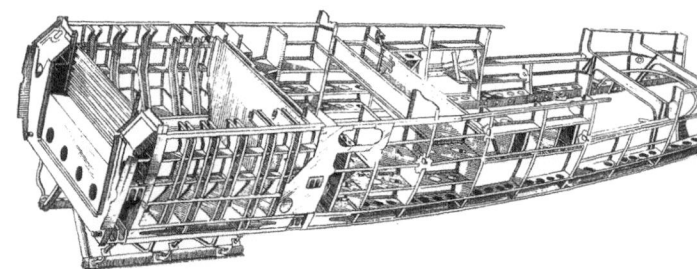

Assembled and skinned separately, the upper and lower fuselage sections allowed for easy installation of control brackets, wiring, flooring, radio parts, and other accessories. Then, the pieces were joined together. According to Republic, "the skin is staggered to facilitate splicing and to avoid too great a strain on the ship at the splice point." *Cradle of Aviation Museum*

wings and supported by the aft wing spar. The motion was then transferred to an aileron drive link that moved the control surface.

The rudder pedals were attached to a series of cables and pulleys that ran aft to the control horns affixed to the rudder's torque tube.

Small trim wheels located on the pilot's left side controlled the trim tabs incorporated on each surface except the right aileron. Adjustment commands traveled mechanically to the tabs via a series of cables, rods, pulleys, chains, and screw actuators.

Electrical System

The P-47's electrical system controlled the intercooler doors, propeller controls, starter, water-injection pump, oil cooler shutter motor, fuel tank pumps, instruments, radio, gun sight, machine gun solenoids, and lights. On later bubble-canopy versions of the fighter, an electric motor opened and closed the canopy. A switch box and circuit breakers on the left side of the cockpit allowed the pilot to control the systems.

Electrical power (twenty-four–volt DC) came from a generator mounted aft of the engine or a storage battery when the engine was off. The battery was likewise housed in the engine compartment along with the induction vibrator, engine starter, and firewall and battery junction boxes.

Hydraulic System

The fighter's landing gear, cowl flaps, and landing flaps were all actuated by the hydraulic system. Located in the engine compartment, a pump driven by the engine powered the hydraulics. Other parts of the system included an equalizer valve (to ensure that both landing flaps were deployed or retracted in unison), a reservoir tank, and a hand pump on the pilot's lower left side in case the hydraulic pump failed.

Each cockpit control lever, for landing gear, cowl flaps, or landing flaps, activated one or more actuating cylinders, causing the desired action. The pilot could pressurize each cylinder, using the hand pump, if the engine-driven pump failed.

When a P-47 flyer experienced a hydraulic failure on takeoff, it was common for his squadron mates to fly a safe distance away and make fun of the afflicted pilot as he pumped furiously to retract his landing gear, his plane's wings waggling as he put all of his effort into pounding the lever over and over. One flyer sarcastically stated that he was almost to the front lines in France before he was able to get the gear all the way up when pumping by hand.

Armament

The army requested that Republic's fighter carry at least six guns, preferably eight. By careful design and arrangement of the landing gear and wing, Kartveli and his team created room for four Browning .50-caliber machine guns and ammunition in each wing of the heavy-hitting fighter.

The guns were staggered within the wings, their breeches between the front and aft main wing spars. The barrels of the guns poked through holes in the forward spar and out the leading edge of the wing.

Ammunition was stowed in the wing outboard of the gun bay, the forward-most ammunition belt feeding the inboard gun, and so on, staggered aft. Ejection-chute holes in the bottom surface of the wing were likewise staggered with the guns.

Each gun could carry a maximum of 425 rounds of ammunition in its bay. More often, around 2,400 rounds were loaded—about 300 per gun. All eight guns fired simultaneously when the pilot pushed the button on the control stick. The typical ammunition load would give the flyer about twenty seconds of firing time. There was no round counter in the cockpit, so armorers sometimes strung a line of tracer bullets at the end of each belt; seeing a steady stream of glowing bullets zip out in front of the nose, a pilot knew he was near the last of his ammunition.

The machine guns were commonly adjusted to converge at a spot about 250 yards in front of the Thunderbolt. This allowed maximum hitting power at a typical speed, altitude, and distance.

Early newspaper articles quote a claim made by enthusiastic Republic engineers that the kinetic energy contained in a burst from the Thunderbolt's guns was equal to that necessary for lifting the 45,000-ton battleship *North Carolina* and a good-sized cruiser completely out of the ocean!

Pilots noted that firing the guns significantly affected the speed of the fighter. The recoil from the machine guns was said to be "about 400 horsepower in the wrong direction," according to one flyer. It was certainly one reason for short, accurate bursts when chasing a fleeing enemy aircraft. Another was that prolonged blasts would "burn up the barrels" of the guns, making subsequent firing highly inaccurate. In the most extreme cases, the guns would become so hot that bullets inside the breeches would "cook off" on their own until the barrels had cooled.

Early models of the Thunderbolt could carry a single 500-pound bomb on their belly pylons. Later versions were equipped with wing pylons to heft bombs or fuel tanks interchangeably. These pylons could hold 1,000-pound bombs, but more frequently squadrons employed a single 500-pound "egg" under each wing. The munitions were dropped electrically, with a mechanical release used as a backup system.

Starting with the late P-47D model series, the Thunderbolt could also haul and launch ten 5-inch high-velocity aircraft rockets (HVARs). Due to the rocket's effectiveness in combat, some earlier models of the fighter received rocket kits as well.

To record the destruction wrought by machine guns and rockets, a gun camera was located in the right wing leading edge. A toggle switch in the cockpit enabled the camera to function with or independently of the guns. Thunderbolt pilots say that originally, when the guns and camera were linked, the camera simply recorded while the trigger was depressed. Later, an adjustment allowed the camera to continue shooting film for approximately five seconds after the pilot released the trigger.

This photograph, showing the amazing firepower of the Jug, often appeared in Republic press releases. The plane was actually photographed on the ground, during a night firing exercise. The Thunderbolt's landing gear was skillfully touched out of the image. *The Museum of Flight*

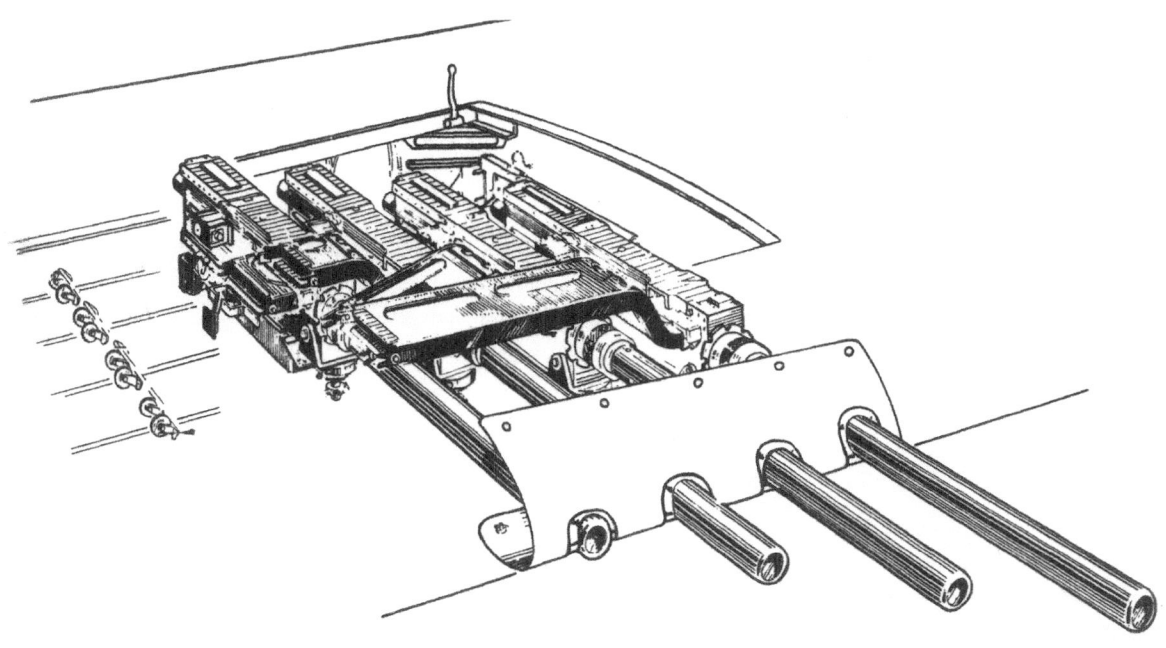

With four Browning .50-caliber machine guns in each wing, the Thunderbolt had immense punching power: thirteen pounds of lead per second! The guns were staggered to allow efficient feeding from the ammunition trays located in the outboard wing. *Cradle of Aviation Museum*

THE COCKPIT

The P-47 cockpit was similar to that of the smaller P-43. Republic struck upon a good design, and the army found little need to change it in the P-47. (Interestingly, the first P-47 from the Republic factory had a side door, similar to Bell's P-39 Airacobra. No one is sure why this change was incorporated; production Thunderbolts emerged from the factory with the standard system.) Both Allied and Axis pilots agreed that the Thunderbolt's cockpit was unusually large. British pilots are reported to have mused that one might dodge enemy bullets simply by keeping the shoulder straps loose and leaning this way and that. A German flyer who peeked inside a captured Thunderbolt reportedly exclaimed that, since the pilot's space was so roomy, perhaps American flyers risked breaking a leg if they slipped from the bucket seat.

Pilots commented that the cockpit was much quieter than those of most other fighter planes of the era. One Long Island flyer who had flown a P-47, as well as Grumman's F6F Hellcat and Vought's F4U Corsair, related that "the deep, muffled, faraway exhaust noise sounded more like that of a Cadillac than of a fighter."

Ready to fire, the guns of a P-47 Thunderbolt await a mission over enemy territory. The sign was hung from the blast tubes to notify ground crews of the danger of eight fully functional .50-caliber machine guns. *National Archives*

A Thunderbolt gets loaded up for a ground attack mission with belts of .50-caliber ammunition and a 500-pound bomb affixed to each wing pylon. A trolley jack is used to lift the high-explosive "egg" into its shackles. *Stan Piet*

Armorers feed some of the most successful guns in the European Theater—those of Francis "Gabby" Gabreski. He flew his P-47 Thunderbolt to victory over twenty-eight aerial foes. From the tally on the side of his aircraft, it seems he was pretty far along when this photo was taken. Like many Thunderbolt flyers, it was attacking ground targets that finally brought him down. He spent the rest of the war in a POW camp. *Stan Piet*

Later D versions of the fighter did away with the raised turtle deck behind the pilot. These early versions, called "razorbacks" by the flyers, limited rearward visibility—the quadrant from where a fighter pilot is most vulnerable. The later aircraft carried a bubble-style canopy on a more cigar-shaped fuselage. Interestingly, this change affected the lateral stability of the aircraft. The problem was corrected by the addition of a dorsal fin, running from the base of the leading edge of the vertical stabilizer forward along the uppermost part of the fuselage.

Inside the cockpit, the Thunderbolt was equipped with a multitude of standard instruments and controls. The instrument panel, forward of the pilot, carried

In the field, a crew chief changes the film in a P-47's gun camera. The camera allowed for many pilots to come home with an accurate record of the destruction they wrought—at least in the Mediterranean and Europe. In the Pacific, much of the film suffered in the humid conditions. *The Museum of Flight, American Fighter Aces collection*

circular gauges, including altimeter, air speed indicator, fuel, compass, tachometer and hydraulic, fuel, manifold, and oxygen-pressure read-outs. On either side of the cockpit were located various switches and levers within easy reach of the pilot.

Directly in front of the pilot was the gun sight. Early P-47s carried the model N-3A, which featured an illuminated circular reticle that allowed the flyer to judge a target's distance and aim his guns. Many later-version P-47s were equipped with the K-14 gyroscopic sight. This improved accuracy, especially when the flyer attempted high-angle deflection shots.

Various SCR-type radio models were used in versions of the P-47 Thunderbolt. The pilot spoke into the radio with the aid of a throat mike and a push-to-talk button on the engine throttle handle on the left side of the cockpit. The transmitter and receivers were located in the fighter's baggage compartment in the rear fuselage. The pilot could operate the radio through switches and dials on his right side.

The transmitter worked in voice mode, continuous wave (CW), and modulated CW settings. There were three receivers, one for each type of transmission. The range of radio frequencies was commonly 201 to 398 kilocycles. Tactical communications ranged from 2,500 to 7,700 kilocycles.

Before every U.S. Army airplane went to the dull olive drab paint scheme of war, this artist painted silver Thunderbolts cruising in the stratosphere. Note that the aircraft carry the prewar national insignia with the red circle in the center. This was dropped in the spring of 1942 to avoid confusion with the Japanese Hinomaru insignia. *Edward Young*

An RC-96 controller transmitter, nicknamed "pip squeak," radiated a signal once a minute, relating the fighter's location and showing it as an Allied aircraft. An SCR-535 identification, friend or foe (IFF) radio set was likewise installed in the baggage compartment. A pilot could press a pair of red buttons in the cockpit near his right elbow to explode the IFF internally to keep the valuable secret radio equipment from enemy hands should the plane be forced down.

Cockpit cooling was supplied by push-pull control on the right side of the pilot. More important was heat, once the fighter was airborne. The pilot's manual for the Thunderbolts says, "Adequate heat is supplied by a hot air type defroster which has a control mounted on the right side of the cockpit just behind the windshield." In reality, pilots say that the heating was anything but adequate. At altitude over Europe, where it was minus sixty degrees Fahrenheit outside, the temperature rarely climbed above zero degrees in the cockpit.

Razorback versions of the fighter carried oxygen bottles in the turtle deck behind the pilot's head. In bubble-canopy P-47s, the bottles were relocated to the leading edge of the wing root, just forward of the front wing spar. The oxygen was supplied to the pilot's mask

Both Allied and Axis fighter pilots were amazed at the P-47's roomy cockpit. The throttle quadrant is visible on the left side of the compartment. Front and center, on the instrument panel, is a placard with safe diving speeds. *National Archives*

Famous P-47 ace Francis "Gabby" Gabreski models the oxygen mask used by Thunderbolt pilots at high altitude. Pilots say you shaved before you flew—stubble would chafe under the mask. They also mention that the tight-fitting mask, along with the helmet, often caused headaches. *National Archives*

through a hose and quick disconnect fitting in the cockpit. Flow, pressure, and valve controls for the system were located on the lower right side of the instrument panel.

Hypoxia, inadequate oxygen in the body's tissues, was a real concern among flyers. Constantly operating above twelve thousand feet, improper oxygen flow or an ice-fouled mask could spell death. Pilots were taught to pull their gloves off in the cold confines of the cockpit and observe their fingernails. Bluish nails were a sure sign of oxygen deprivation.

In abbreviated English, the pilot's manual for the Thunderbolt says, "Front and rear armor protection sufficient to withstand U.S. .30, German .312, and Japanese and Italian .303 (7.7mm)-caliber fire by direct right angle hit is provided for the pilot." The large R-2800 engine protected the bulk of a pilot's body, and a 3/8-inch-thick, face-hardened armor plate located forward of the instrument panel covered a flyer's upper torso. The front panel

of the plane's windscreen was made from 1 1/2-inch-thick bullet-resistant glass. From behind, a large sheet of face-hardened armor plating extended from behind the pilot's head to his rear end in the bucket seat. In bubble-canopy versions of the P-47, this plate narrowed at the shoulders, giving the pilot a favorable view to his six o'clock position. Secondary L-shaped pieces of armor plate protected the side profile of the Thunderbolt's fuel tanks. There was no side armor plate for the pilot.

As a company ad proudly proclaimed, "Prodigious in heft and brawn, supreme in speed and punch, squadrons of 2,000-h.p. Republic P-47 Thunderbolts excel in sheer destructive power. No altitude is too great, no enemy too fast or too strong, for these stalwart fighting units of the U.S. Army Air Forces." It was a big reputation to live up to. It was fighting words. But it was now nearly time to turn words into action.

Nearing the door, D-model Thunderbolts receive their cowlings, propellers, and canopies before test flights. Note the dolly system on the floor to easily move the planes forward. *National Archives*

Thunderbolt upper fuselage sections receive their aluminum skin as they move slowly toward completion. Actually, "slowly" is a relative term: sixteen or seventeen airframes came though this area *each day* at the height of production. *National Archives*

CHAPTER THREE
THE HOME FRONT: THE BATTLE TO BUILD P-47s

The P-47 served practically everywhere during World War II, in part because so many of the type were produced. The battle to build the Thunderbolt at three different factories was paramount to the plane's success in combat. Like the fighting in Europe and the Pacific, the war at home was complex and multi-faceted, filled with victories and defeats that translated directly to those flying the Thunderbolt overseas.

REPUBLIC, PREWAR

In late 1940, Republic Aviation Corporation, based at Farmingdale, Long Island, in New York State, operated a mid-sized factory run by a small, tight-knit community of fewer than five thousand workers. *Republic Aviation News*, published for the employees, gives a sense of the peacetime life led by those in the company, who called themselves the RACers. (RAC stood for Republic Aviation Corporation.)

In the Christmas issue of 1940 is a section under the heading of "If We Were Santa Claus, We Would Give." The desires for the RACers were fairly simple: "a new switchboard for Lil and Jeanette, better ventilation to the Offices, and better attendance and facilities for the Republic employee sports teams."

Indeed, the on-the-field battles with Republic's Long Island rival, Grumman Aircraft Engineering Corporation, often got much of the ink in those early days. The RACer teams, usually named the Aviators, fought the dreaded Grumman Bombers in every arena—basketball, baseball, softball, bowling—the blow-by-blow described in the company newspaper the following week.

A regular column, Republicapers, by "Jimmy Jig" carried inside jokes overheard in the factory, poems, and funny stories. Propwash and Things and Stuff described the comings and goings and major life milestones of individual Republic employees. Men from the company's major customer, the army, were treated like part of the family, with the RACers poking fun at the chubby AAF men, wishing for "less tempting menus for certain officers trying to diet." Other wishes included "lots of P-43s for Captain Keillor" and "lots of overtime for everybody"; that last wish was certainly granted.

War was coming, and life around the plant was changing. In January 1941, the company erected a fence

The frontispiece for a wartime employment handbook entitled *You and Your Job at Republic Aviation Corporation* shows the massive Building 17, a male and female worker, and a smiling combat pilot. Note the Republic logo, with distinctive, elliptical-winged fighters. *Cradle of Aviation Museum*

around the factory, shutting out the public. Employees received photo identification badges for the first time. Security personnel began fingerprinting new employees and manning the gates as workers came and went from their shifts.

To build P-43s, ground was broken on a massive new plant on January 10, 1941. (The final deal, inked a few weeks before, was called "Uncle Sam's Christmas gift to Republic.") It was a $5.2 million-dollar job that would increase the company workspace by 780,000 square feet, require thousands of new workers, and "bring increased responsibility to all who are now employed at the Corporation," reported company officials. There were $2.5 million worth of government orders on the line and the potential for a lot more as the war in Europe intensified.

On May 6, the airplane known by Gen. Henry "Hap" Arnold as "the X job" was ready. About 150 RACers stopped work to see their newest creation, the XP-47B,

take wing. Test pilot Lowery Brabham taxied the company's biggest, newest monster onto the newly extended but still unpaved, puddle-filled field. He ran up the R-2800 engine, and globs of mud and grass and water spray went flying.

It was the defining moment for the company, though few probably knew it at the time. Republic's chances of survival, growth, and longevity rode with that single silver beast. And, looking back, the battle plans and combat effectiveness of a nation, soon to be embroiled in a worldwide conflict, were suddenly in the hands of a single man, a former country fair barnstormer and stunt pilot who had gone on to the army and then into civil flying.

"Brab," as everyone called him, released the brakes. A few seconds later, the Thunderbolt, America's newest super-fighter, clawed into the air. After a few passes, the plane rumbled out of sight. "Gosh, how exciting," the

The XP-47B Thunderbolt flew for the first time on May 6, 1941. The plane carried hardly any markings. Mostly bare metal besides the rudder and yellow trim tab, the new fighter had "U.S. ARMY" painted in black on the underside of its wings. *Stan Piet*

RACers said as they went back to work on the P-43 line.

It was "exciting" in a much different way for Brabham as he cruised west. The cockpit was filling with smoke—heavy, black, oily clouds. The prototype Thunderbolt had no sliding canopy as such, so Brab opened the small side window, which made things even worse. Blinded and choking, he thought of bailing out, but he realized that the loss of this plane would be a disaster to Republic. "I solved the problem by not breathing much, and that first touchdown at Mitchel Field felt pretty good," he later wrote.

Republic had arranged to have the Thunderbolt land at Mitchel, an army airfield, because of the lousy condition of the Farmingdale field. The new plane attracted quite a crowd of curious army types until pushed into a hangar.

The cockpit smoke proved minor: oil leaking down from the exhaust pipes into the turbocharger, which was not run during engine tests on the ground. Brabham phoned his superiors and told them, "Boy, we've hit the jackpot!"

Days later, the army accepted the plane into full production. Most regular front-line RACers, however, were still focused on setting up the new factory building and producing P-43 Lancers. By October 1941, the first P-43s emerged from the new plant. The army wanted $67.5 million worth of P-43s and P-47s from Republic, which raised the company's backlog to over $100 million.

The huge orders, combined with the U.S. entry into World War II, prompted the *Republic Aviation News* of December 23, 1941, to remark, "Good luck, Merry Christmas, Happy New Year, we start around-the-clock, seven-days-a-week work on Monday. The big push is on—for us all."

THE PLANT

Building 17 was huge. Financed by the U.S. government, the giant assembly plant ultimately cost $3 million to erect and contained $3 million more worth of shops and equipment to build large, high-altitude fighters.

A railway platform on the west side handled an eight-car train carrying a plethora of raw materials, supplies, and subcontracted assemblies made offsite. On the east end, eight hundred feet away, large doors opened to roll out finished planes to Republic's expanded 240-acre flying field. The building boasted forty-two continuous rows of fluorescent lights five hundred feet long and spaced twenty-two feet apart. Exhaust and supply fans

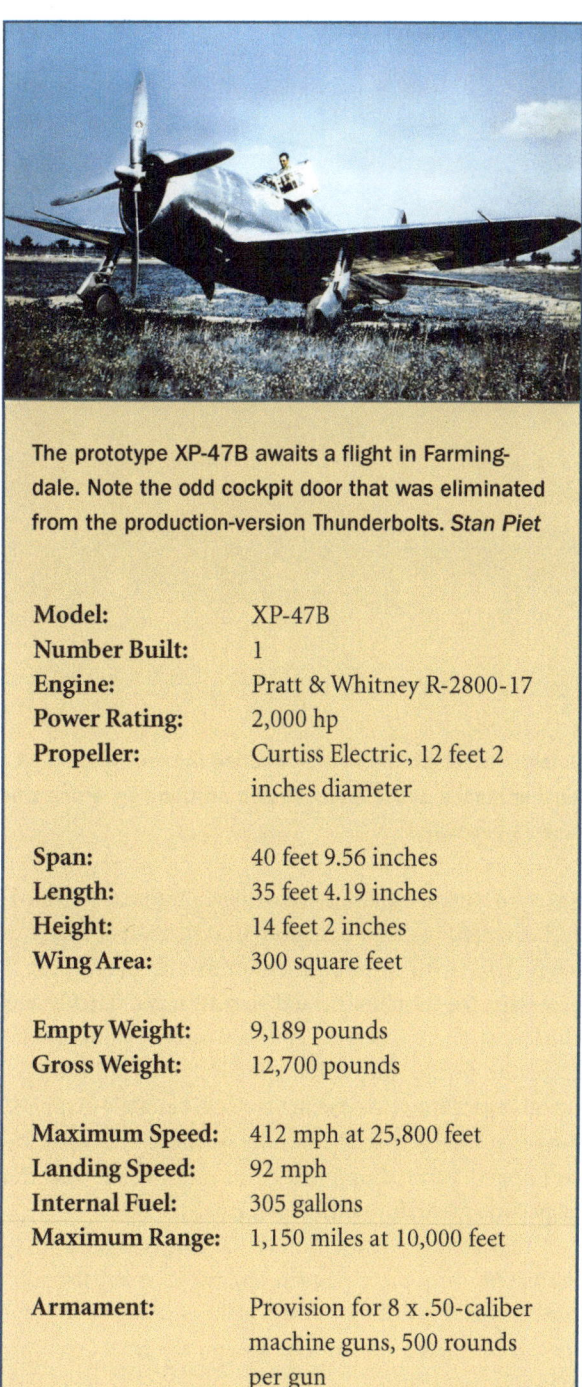

The prototype XP-47B awaits a flight in Farmingdale. Note the odd cockpit door that was eliminated from the production-version Thunderbolts. *Stan Piet*

Model:	XP-47B
Number Built:	1
Engine:	Pratt & Whitney R-2800-17
Power Rating:	2,000 hp
Propeller:	Curtiss Electric, 12 feet 2 inches diameter
Span:	40 feet 9.56 inches
Length:	35 feet 4.19 inches
Height:	14 feet 2 inches
Wing Area:	300 square feet
Empty Weight:	9,189 pounds
Gross Weight:	12,700 pounds
Maximum Speed:	412 mph at 25,800 feet
Landing Speed:	92 mph
Internal Fuel:	305 gallons
Maximum Range:	1,150 miles at 10,000 feet
Armament:	Provision for 8 x .50-caliber machine guns, 500 rounds per gun

changed the air in the building six times an hour. A 250,000-gallon storage tank supported sprinklers and fire pumps.

Other buildings on the sprawling Republic site, about fifteen in all, were retained as offices, warehouses, machine shops, and experimental and engineering facili-

Outside the plant, the first production model Thunderbolt awaits test flights from Republic's Farmingdale airfield. A fire extinguisher stands at the ready, should anything go wrong when the big Double Wasp was brought to life. *The Museum of Flight, Bowers collection*

ties. While these buildings were often cluttered, cramped, and divided, the new assembly building was primarily open space with minimum columns and partitions. If necessary, the shop floor could be rearranged quickly and efficiently. There was one significant and very intentional exception to the rule, which effectively divided the cavernous space into two distinct areas. A carefully arranged bottleneck existed in the middle of the space, with the large-parts paint shop jutting out on one side and the inspection laboratory pushing in from the other.

This arrangement ensured that inspectors carefully evaluated every piece of each aircraft as it left the subassembly and detail part of the plant (the west end) and moved through a fifteen-foot aisle to the final assembly area (the east end).

The west end was a series of five bays, each of which was one hundred feet wide, with a clerestory height up to twenty feet. This was a seemingly never-ending landscape of tool shops, stock rooms, huge pieces of manufacturing equipment (including a massive 4,500-pound press), rows of work tables, stacks and racks holding parts of every kind, and large, complex jigs to fix components in place as they were assembled.

It took about twenty-eight thousand fabricated parts, supplied by the company's own production and its 480 subcontractors in twenty-four different states, to make a single Thunderbolt. Parts came from far and wide. Some vendors were familiar to aviation, such as Pratt & Whitney, American Magnesium Corporation, Aluminum Company of America, United Aircraft, and Bendix Aviation Corporation. Other suppliers for the Thunderbolt were companies who had obviously switched their focus somewhat to help in the war effort. Among these were the Maytag Corporation, Minnesota Mining and Manufacturing Company, Shakeproof Incorporated, the Aluminum Cooking Utensil Company, Armstrong Cork Company, and S. S. White Dental Manufacturing Company.

Proud to assist, these firms often carried an image of a fire-spitting P-47 on the covers of wartime issues of their company newsletters—whether it be the Otis Elevator Employees' *Yonkers Works Digest, The Coltsman News* from Colt's Firearm Company, or the monthly tome *Michigan Seamless Tube-Tips.* One corporation, making small parts for Republic's "deadly sky predator," had manufactured eye beauty products before the fighting began.

On the subassembly side of the factory, a Republic worker puts the finishing touches on a new bubble canopy shipped from a subcontractor. Earlier Thunderbolt models had a "birdcage" style canopy and high rear fuselage, which obstructed a flyer's view of the sky around him. The new system allowed for much better vision in nearly every direction. *Cradle of Aviation Museum*

New fuselages, lined up on the final assembly side of Building 17, await their turn to be mated to wings in 1943. In the center of the factory floor, nearly complete Thunderbolts slowly make their way down the line toward the east doors. Seeing Republic's line not populated with workers was a rarity; an army photographer must have shot this photo at a break or shift change. *National Archives*

As the PR people at Republic wrote, "Our subcontractors and suppliers have functioned almost like branch factories. They have met—and overcame—difficulties that in peacetime might have seemed insurmountable. And joined with Republic in one tremendous effort."

The subcontractors' labors—clear canopies from Lear, struts from Cleveland Pneumatic Tool, oil coolers from Young Radiator, and thousands upon thousands of other devices, components, and parts, arrived at the loading docks and railway platform of Building 17 in an almost endless stream. The parts were combined with materials created on-site by Republic's own employees to make up the major subassemblies of the P-47: upper and lower fuselage, tail cone, engine group, tail group, wing sections, and so forth.

When these large sections of aircraft were completed, they left the never-ending din of the whirring drills, popping rivet guns, the crackle of welding units, and humming presses for the bottleneck area between the west and east sides of the plant. There, company and army inspectors guarded the corridor, looking over every piece, ensuring it was up to standard in specification, tooling, fabrication, and assembly. Only after it was passed by these men and women, was it allowed through to the east side of Building 17—final assembly.

Monorails, overhead trolleys, and electrical and mechanical hoists helped move the parts into position on the east side. Here, the pace was equally hectic and noisy as employees joined fuselages, mounted engines, affixed tail and wing sections, and positioned each new plane on its gear for the first time. As each behemoth moved along, it looked more and more recognizable as a Thunderbolt with each passing day. The final assembly lines terminated near the two-hundred-foot-long and thirty-five-foot-wide canopy doors on the extreme east end of the shop.

RACers seldom paused to watch their creations placed on the scales and towed outside to a nearby hangar for flight tests and final acceptance. They commonly turned away to dive in with their ratchets and rivet guns on the next Thunderbolt in the line. A huge banner hung over the doors urged, "KEEP THAT LINE ROLLING." When the assembly line was running smoothly, the pace at which Republic could turn out these seven-ton metal monsters was simply astounding.

INDIANA'S RAIDERS

It wasn't enough for the army. Their need for the P-47 Thunderbolt was so great that, in the early months of 1942, the U.S. Army Air Forces (AAF) had asked Republic to create a second source as quickly as possible to churn out more of the badly needed fighters.

The location of the new facility was a secret. But at this early stage in the war, the smart money was inland, somewhere less vulnerable to attack. German U-boats were sinking ships right off the coast. Rumors were swirling in the newspapers about German bombing attacks planned for New York City and East Coast aircraft facilities.

A shortwave radio station in Centerport, Long Island, had intercepted eerie transmissions: "How many Curtiss P-40s are being produced monthly? How many Allison motors are being currently delivered to Lockheed and Bell? Armament details and deliveries of Grumman fighters F4F?" These were questions for Nazi spies within the aviation community.

Republic was included in the long list of queries. "How many fighter planes ordered by Sweden?" referring to P-35 type fighters de Seversky had convinced the country to acquire in 1939 and 1940. The answer was 120 planes. "How many of this order goes to England?" Answer: None. Republic has something else headed to England. You'll be seeing them soon.

To say the least, it was an uncertain time. The notion that the single Thunderbolt factory at Farmingdale could be wiped off the map by a German surprise attack or saboteur was enough to convince Republic and the army to look for a spot much harder to reach than Long Island. Republic announced, "Somewhere in Indiana," and only later was a cornfield near Evansville finally designated as the new home for Republic's Indiana Division.

While some at Farmingdale were drawing up plans and procuring equipment for Evansville, most were building P-47s day after day. The seventh P-47B on the line at Farmingdale was the company's gift to the army. The company's employees purchased the fighter with war bonds and worked on the machine while they were off the clock. By March, it was finished and Assistant Secretary of War for Air Robert A. Lovett was on hand to accept the aircraft, dubbed *Lucky Seven*, on behalf of the army. Months later, the plane was reported in action in the Far East.

Ready to fly seven miles high, a Republic test pilot wears his heavy sheepskin and leather flight suit, an oxygen mask, and a Mae West life preserver, just in case. Strapped to his right leg is a knee board with notes about flight parameters. *National Archives*

Republic employees purchased war bonds at a furious rate. The twenty-first war bond Thunderbolt, which voluntary payroll deductions paid for, went to the army's 353rd Fighter Group of the Eighth Air Force. Here, the fighter is seen in England with "Slybird" squadron pilot Lt. D. J. Corrigan and his crew chief. Interestingly, the flyer preferred British-style goggles and a rearview mirror similar to those mounted on Spitfircs. *National Archives*

In April, the first spades of earth were turned on the plot of land in Indiana, followed by a get-acquainted dinner with leading citizens in Evansville. Only five months later, Republic brass were back to celebrate the opening of full production. Planes were rolling out while the factory went up around them.

At the celebration, a Farmingdale Thunderbolt and a new plane from Evansville named *Hoosier Spirit* were flown for the crowd. An army general in charge of the AAF Material Center told the gathered workers that the two plants together were going to build more airplanes in the following year than the entire American industry could manage just three years before. Republic president Ralph Damon promised the AAF that all the planes scheduled to be delivered by Christmas 1942 by the new

plant would be completed by Columbus Day (October 12). And he kept his promise, thanks to the amazing efficiency of the Indiana workers, who called themselves the Raiders.

THE PEOPLE

In wartime, Republic's pool of workers increased immensely, from fewer than 200 in 1939 to 24,450 at the height of production in 1944. These gains were made despite young employees of draft age being pulled away to serve in the armed forces. Some 1,084 was the count in late 1942 of those who had left to join the military. By mid-1943, 2,341 had left the company to take a more direct role in the armed struggle. In March 1945 the number was 4,242. It was reported that sixteen of the men had been killed in action.

So the company sought others around Long Island and in Indiana to make up the difference and much more. The company looked to older workers, including an elderly cobbler who had spent his life cutting shapes from leather while creating minimum waste. His skills translated directly to planning cuts in aluminum sheets, minimizing scrap. There were also several hundred veterans from World War I and more than six hundred returning GIs discharged from military service welcomed into the fold.

A New York State industrial commissioner commented to the *Brooklyn Eagle* newspaper that "Hundreds of employers in this State who have discriminated against qualified workers because they were Negroes or Jewish or of Italian or German extraction are today reversing their practice," as war production ramped up. It certainly was a different time.

Republic also hired women workers. In a previously male-dominated field, thousands of Long Island females reported to the factory. "Many of them are wives, mothers, sisters, or daughters of men in the Nation's armed services," explained Republic's annual report. The company had the largest percentage of women workers of any defense contractor at one point in the war, around 60 percent. "Some of the most difficult and delicate jobs on the Republic assembly line are performed by women workers, without whose intelligent, patriotic service Republic's production records could never have been achieved," the PR men stated.

Pilots on both sides of the fight recognized that the Thunderbolt was a brute, a monster, a beast—but it was built by ladies. And when a mighty P-47 was finished at

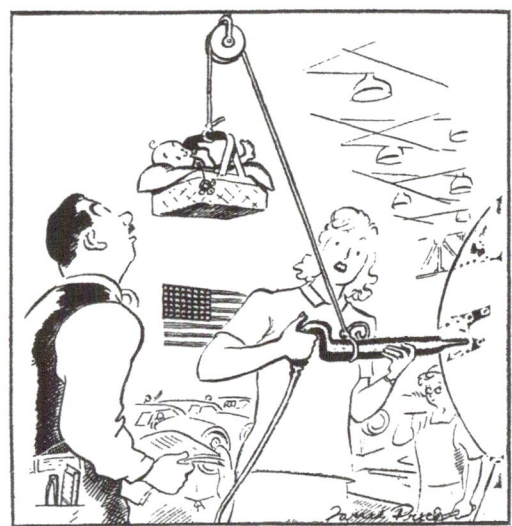

"It Not Only Amuses the Baby—It Makes This Dingbat Easier to Lift."

Women in the workplace were a new reality for many veteran aircraft manufacturers. As young men went off to war, companies recruited females to take their place on the factory floor. This Republic cartoon makes fun of a woman's natural ability to multitask. *Cradle of Aviation Museum*

Women pilots flew nearly every plane in the American inventory during the war, including four-engine heavy bombers and the biggest, baddest fighters. Here, a WASP gets ready to ferry a Thunderbolt from an army airfield. Note the streamlined rearview mirror on top of the canopy. *Stan Piet*

Farmingdale, the biggest, heaviest single-engine fighter in America's arsenal was often flown away from the factory by a young woman—a member of the U.S. Army's Women's Airforce Service Pilot (WASP) program.

In a time of war, most Republic employees were good-hearted and generous. A part-time worker, a mother of four children, lost an envelope containing her entire week's pay in the lunchroom. In a matter of minutes, her co-workers had chipped in enough money to more than make up for the loss. The RACers worked overtime and donated money to buy war bonds at a terrific rate. They often worked through their vacation days. Everyone was there on Labor Day, hammering away at the planes.

Republic rewarded employees who offered suggestions to save time and money on the Thunderbolt line with fifty-dollar war bonds. On one occasion, the com-

Republic workers rap rivets into the upper fuselage skin of a Thunderbolt-to-be at Farmingdale. Workers inside the fuselage held up a heavy metal bucking bar to smash the end of the rivets and hold them in place after they were pounded. It must have been an uncomfortable and terribly noisy job. *Cradle of Aviation Museum*

pany recognized a worker who had created a new type of bucking bar to help rivet the air scoop in the nose. The device saved ten hours per plane. Another man invented an instrument dubbed the "revoclock." It helped set the limit switches on the oil cooler door mechanism. Time saved: seven hours for each plane.

The company led by example. When Republic delivered all of the P-43 Lancer fighters and parts to the army,

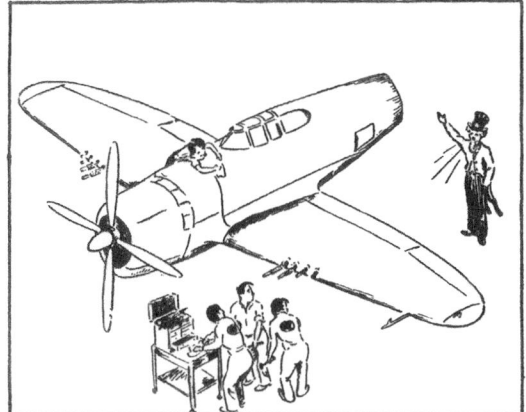

ABSENT WORKER—ABSENT SHIP   by Milt

"Say, fellows, where is the rest of the ship?"

"There it is! The Sunday absentees are running off with it."
—Drawn from idea submitted by L. F. Malek.

The Republic factory sometimes was up and running seven days a week. One of its most significant problems was absenteeism, especially on Sundays. This comic, appealing to worker's sense of patriotism, ran in the *Republic Aviation News* in 1942. *Cradle of Aviation Museum*

we are cheating [those men on the front lines.]" He called the dawdling "treason"—and you could be shot for treason.

One of the biggest problems at Republic was absenteeism on Sundays. Factory workers were frustrated that the office people seemed to get more time off. But, explained the company, "it is vital that a milling machine of fuselage jig be kept busy seven days a week. There aren't enough of them to go round. Time is short. The important thing is to do our assigned jobs, not to be a cry-baby or to worry about the other fellow's job. Victory is our business."

Another dominant issue was safety. Thousands of people who had never worked a factory job before were now operating hundreds of machines that could, in a moment's inattention, zip off their fingers and never even slow down. Besides their own safety, workers had to consider the pilot flying the plane overseas. Posters every-

Released to the army's PR bureau in April 1944, this photo shows bare-metal D-model Thunderbolts lined up for delivery to units overseas. Through combat operations, accidents, and heavy use, fighting squadrons estimated they went through around 30 percent of their P-47 fighters every month during wartime. *National Archives*

the company had done the job for $1.4 million less than planned and returned the funds to the U.S. government.

There were a few bad apples, of course. Slackers made people's blood boil more than anything else. The Republic company paper published a letter from a factory worker at Douglas Aircraft in California. The worker noted that while young men were dying in places like Wake Island and Guam, other fellows of the same age seemed to be dragging their feet at factory jobs. "Every minute we let up to talk to the fellow on the next bench, to loaf in the wash room, to sneak a forbidden cigarette, where hammered the message home: "How important is this small part? THINK. If the threads are stripped then the part becomes useless." Failure to properly insulate a single wire could start a fire that could lead to the loss of an expensive fighter and a highly trained pilot. And the pilot just might be someone they knew.

Times were hectic; everyone was making sacrifices. The nation was rationing gasoline, oil, coffee, sugar, and meat. To save oil, thermostats in the factory and offices were turned below sixty degrees during the winter of 1943. People were forced to carpool. It was noted that a single air attack on Germany required Allied aircraft to fly an aggregate of 850,000 miles, burning more than one million gallons of fuel. "Yeah, maybe there is something behind this gasoline rationing after all," stated the Republic newspaper.

There were pleasant moments, too. The day hus-

It was a joyous day back home when Thunderbolts were finally reported to have cut their teeth in combat overseas. The line stopped and workers cheered—only briefly. Then, it was back to work with renewed vigor. *Cradle of Aviation Museum*

bands and wives employed at Republic were allowed to move to the same shifts was good. It was even better for the Raiders of Indiana when they received a surprise visit from President Franklin D. Roosevelt.

But best of all was the news that Thunderbolts had entered combat over Europe. The Republic fighters and American pilots had been fighting for nearly a month, but it was May 10, 1943, before word reached home. In a rare moment, workers dropped their tools and danced and cheered and yelled as Republic President Ralph Damon drove from shop to shop on an electric-powered delivery truck, spreading the word.

The celebration lasted about fifteen minutes before people caught themselves and plunged into their jobs with renewed vigor. As one RACer told the *New York Herald Tribune*, "Hitler's going to get his belly full now."

With the P-47's combat debut came fame. Prime Minister Winston Churchill called the Thunderbolt "the world's superfighter." Soldiers in Jersey named a falcon they were training to attack enemy carrier pigeons "Thunderbolt." A P-47 was hoisted through the window of the New York Museum of Science and Industry near Rockefeller Center as part of an AAF exhibition. And a Broadway bar began selling Thunderbolt cocktails to patrons, claiming, "It makes your head spin at 780 miles per hour."

In October came "Family Day," a rare chance for non-workers to see the factory. The RACers jokingly called the event "two thrill-packed miles of factory tours," but it was all new and different for many of the more than 57,000 people who came. A comic in the Republic news showed a middle-aged man uncomfortably dressed in a suit, standing with his wife and children. His attention is focused on a small portion of the tail of a huge Thunderbolt, the bulk of the machine looming behind. "Here's the important part, momma," says the caption, "that I work on."

Indeed, corporate officials encouraged a feeling of pride at Republic. The red, white, and blue cardboard badges used on Family Day carry a photo of the big fighter clawing its way through the skies. Below the image it says, "Republic's P-47 Thunderbolt. The Plane I Help To Build."

THE ROAD TO VICTORY

Hard work paid off. Ahead of their quotas, the men and women of Republic received $1 million in adjusted compensation and incentive bonuses. The plants earned the

Army Navy "E" Production Award many times over. On the first occasion, a female night-shift worker told reporters, "I was so happy I almost hugged the inspector who happened to be standing near me."

In the early part of 1944, the Farmingdale plant was rated at 100.8 percent efficiency. It seemed everyone nearby was working at Republic or Grumman—the workforce even included a doctor of philosophy who turned in her academic robes to rap rivets into P-47s at the Long Island plant.

Evansville was close behind. They were now accounting for 40 percent of all Thunderbolts made. Together, the two factories averaged twenty-eight seven-ton fighters each day. It sounds like a lot, but flying units in Europe figured they needed to replace 20 percent of their Thunderbolts each month—lost in combat, damaged beyond repair in accidents, or simply worn out. They later raised the number to around 30 percent to keep the squadrons full of the fighting Jugs.

The black eye during all of this was the attempt to make Thunderbolts at the Curtiss-Wright plant in Buffalo, New York. In retrospect, it seems that the company did not have enthusiasm for the job. Curtiss was very busy with many projects, and probably would have rather been making more of its own P-40 Warhawk fighters, but that type was becoming obsolete.

Republic officials just scratched their heads. Evansville had no factory at the start of the war, and most of the Indiana men and women had been farm folks. *They* were pounding out thousands of frontline Thunderbolts. The Curtiss people were experienced airplane makers, with a ready factory. They only made 354 Thunderbolts before the army told them to quit.

The planes Curtiss did make were outdated even when they were new. They were commonly kept in the

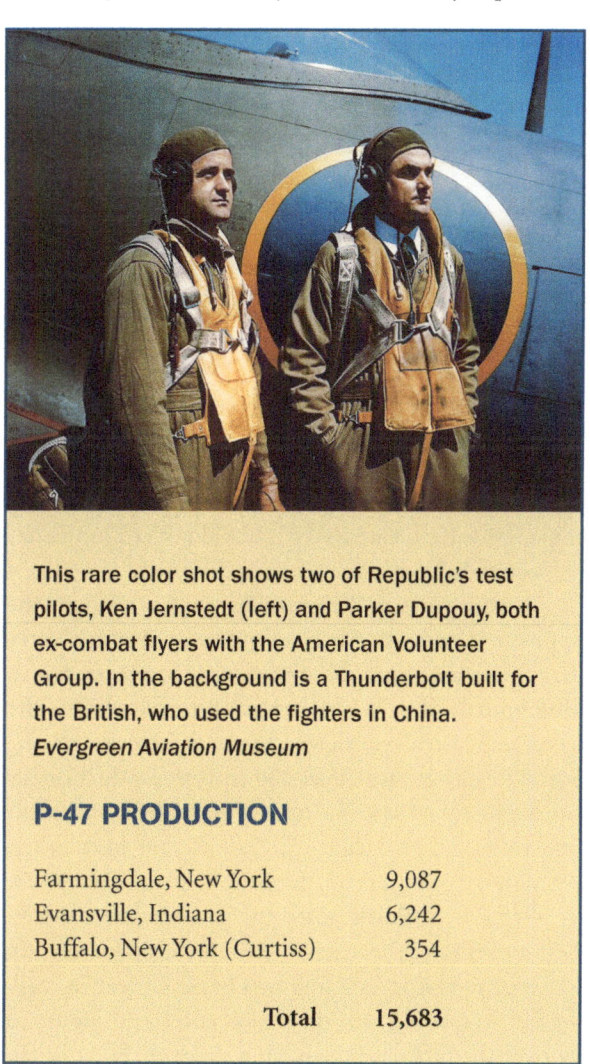

This rare color shot shows two of Republic's test pilots, Ken Jernstedt (left) and Parker Dupouy, both ex-combat flyers with the American Volunteer Group. In the background is a Thunderbolt built for the British, who used the fighters in China. *Evergreen Aviation Museum*

P-47 PRODUCTION

Farmingdale, New York	9,087
Evansville, Indiana	6,242
Buffalo, New York (Curtiss)	354
Total	**15,683**

An army poster says it all—the country needed every P-47 it could put into battle with the enemy. Republic responded with all the government asked for and more, creating the most widely produced American fighter of all time. *Author's collection*

Proud of their achievement—ten thousand Thunderbolts—the *Republic Aviation News* ran this drawing in its September 20, 1944, edition. Indeed, for the enemy, it seemed P-47s were swarming everywhere. *Cradle of Aviation Museum*

United States for training duties. It was enough to drive the War Production Board completely nuts. As students of aviation history know, with the government now distrustful of the company for this awful showing and a few others, Curtiss-Wright did not last long after the war ended.

Farmingdale and Evansville were headed in the opposite direction. Their output was so impressive that the main work shifts were reduced from ten to nine hours a day. When a tropical hurricane hit the East Coast, Farmingdale was the only factory on Long Island to stay at more than 100 percent production. In late September 1944, the ten thousandth Thunderbolt rolled off the line. Jacqueline Cochran, the head of the WASP ferry pilot service, dubbed the plane *Ten Grand*.

Republic officials noted that the ten thousand P-47s would stretch seventy-seven miles if flown wingtip to wingtip. Flying in a line two hundred feet in trail, the fighters would take three days and twelve hours to fly over the factory. It took an average of 22,925 man

hours to make one of the first 773 aircraft. *Ten Grand* took 6,290 man (and woman) hours to build. While one of the first Thunderbolts cost $68,750, the army acquired this plane for $45,600. Beyond the ten thousand aircraft, Republic also produced enough spare parts to make 2,309 additional fighters.

When victory seemed only a matter of months away, there was still tragedy. In October 1944, Republic technical representative Arthur Fowler was killed in a crash in France. He became the first person on Republic's payroll to die in the war.

And there was a small box in the *Republic Aviation News* that read: "Fate played one of its cruelest tricks on the popular Gloria Warren, of the Standards Group of Engineering, last Tuesday. Tuesday was Gloria's twenty-first birthday, the day her husband, Lt. Richard B. Warren, Thunderbolt pilot stationed in England, expected to celebrate, even though he could not spend it with her. But Tuesday she received the fatal Government telegram announcing that he had been killed in action."

Shifts returned to ten-hour days as the P-47N models were readied for the Pacific. Evansville took on the task of making cowlings for the engines of Boeing B-29 Superfortress bombers destined to attack Japan.

As 1945 dawned, Republic received word *Ten Grand* was fighting with a unit in Italy. A flood of the Ohio River and a tornado, both within a ten-day period, failed to stop production in Evansville as it delivered its five thousandth plane. As war wound down in Europe, *Ten Grand* was reported dead—she had brought her pilot back safely to his home base with a 40mm shell in her main spar. The hearty plane had gone through four engine changes, three wing changes, and a new set of elevators before she was declared junk.

Fifteen Grand rolled off the line just ten months after *Ten Grand*. By then, the war in Europe was over and the battles in the Pacific took center stage. The long-range Thunderbolts were flying over downtown Tokyo, but talk remained of a long, bloody invasion of the Japanese home islands.

Two atomic bombs, dropped on the other side of the globe, changed everything for the Republic workers in Evansville and Farmingdale. When Japan surrendered, the news was flashed to the United States during the factories' night "victory shifts." The workers dropped their tools and celebrated. Both plants were ordered to partly shut down for ten days. Finally, the RACers and Raiders got a well-deserved rest.

The final P-47 came off the line a few months later. *Old 444* was an N-model. A photo of the plane appeared on the front of the November 9, 1945, issue of the *Republic Aviation News*. In the image, test pilot Lowery Brabham, the man who flew the first P-47, sits in the cockpit. On the tarmac are a small number of well-wishers—veteran RACers who helped build the first P-47 as well as every Farmingdale Thunderbolt thereafter.

"Jove, Watson! The way I deduce it, Evansville, Indiana, must be the largest place in the world, and everybody there must make Thunderbolts!"

The workers of Evansville, Indiana, were proud of their amazing P-47 production output. The sheer volume of aircraft made by both Republic factories made it possible for army commanders to put hundreds of Thunderbolts in the air for important missions over Europe.
Cradle of Aviation Museum

P-47Cs of the 56th Fighter Group cruise the skies, looking for a fight in 1943. *National Archives*

Shipyard workers unload precious cargo from America: much-needed P-47 Thunderbolts. The planes were carefully offloaded to barges at ports in the U.K. On dry land once again, the fighters were quickly stripped of their protective coating and readied for flight. *National Archives*

CHAPTER FOUR
RAMROD: P-47 FIGHTER ESCORTS

The first P-47s to enter combat transited the Atlantic via ship in late 1942. As young American pilots made their way overseas, perhaps one of them recalled a verse from the King James Bible: "Then shall the right aiming thunderbolts go abroad; and from the clouds, as from a well drawn bow, shall they fly to the mark." The first of their mounts arrived in England a few days before Christmas. The U.S. Army hoped to have three groups of P-47s operational by spring of 1943.

THE FIRST P-47 FIGHTER GROUPS

Not all of the first P-47 pilots were arriving with the aircraft. The 4th Fighter Group was made up of veteran volunteer airmen from Eagle Squadrons. They had been flying and fighting alongside the British even before the United States entered the war.

They loved their small, lithe Supermarine Spitfires. When their commanding officer told them they would soon receive burly Thunderbolts, he added, "But under no account must anything be said about it. It must be kept from the Jerries." One witty flyer retorted, "They'll know soon enough when they see us crashing all over the place!" They waited for the new Republic fighters as if they were coffins.

Most Eagle Squadron pilots, like their British counterparts, were appalled the first time they saw a P-47 Thunderbolt up close. Compared to the Spit, the new plane was a fat, ugly monster. Most historians say the nickname applied nearly universally to the P-47, the Jug, was a shortened version of "Juggernaut." But that wasn't the case in these early days. "She looks like a giant milk jug," blurted one of the Brit airmen. "They've sent seven-ton milk jugs with wings."

Could this monster hold its own against skillful Luftwaffe pilots and their small Focke-Wulfs and Messerschmitts? The task of wringing out the P-47 in the field went to test pilot Maj. Cass Hough, heir to the Daisy BB-gun company. Compared to a captured Focke-Wulf Fw-190A, the Thunderbolt could out-turn and outrun the German fighter at high altitudes. Indeed, the P-47 seemed to thrive in the thin air—the realm for which it was designed.

Below fifteen thousand feet, it was a different story: the 190 was appreciably better, faster, and more maneuverable.

Thunderbolts of the 78th Fighter Group stand ready for combat after being transported to England in late 1942. The army's caption for the photo says that the planes are bound for the Mediterranean, but instead, the 78th stayed put, escorting bombers over occupied Europe. *National Archives*

Pilots took note: no dogfighting down low. Dive down, do your damage, and then zoom-climb upstairs before something blocked your path. It wasn't the most encouraging news.

Because of their own set of circumstances, the two other fighter groups to acquire the first deliveries of Thunderbolts along with the 4th were a bit more happy with the fighters. The 78th Fighter Group had seen most of their Lockheed P-38 Lightnings and many of their pilots dispatched to units in North Africa. They were simply pleased to be back in business and anxious to tear into the Germans, though somewhat wary of their new mounts.

The third unit, the 56th Fighter Group, had flown the Thunderbolt before. They were the first operational P-47 unit in the United States and were destined to become the most successful Thunderbolt outfit overseas. Because of their stateside experience, they were the least apprehensive of the three.

Since the newcomers' P-47s looked somewhat like the German Focke-Wulf from certain angles, each unit prepared for battle by painting white stripes on their tails and a thick white band around the nose cowlings.

Problems with the Jug's engine, creating noisy interference on the plane's radio system, delayed entry into combat until April 15, 1943. On that milestone day, pilots led by Maj. Don Blakeslee of the 4th Fighter Group spied a group of German 190s over the coast of Belgium. The Jugs were at twenty-nine thousand feet and the 190s about five thousand feet lower. The enemy

pilots spotted the Thunderbolts and turned toward home. The Americans went down after them.

Blakeslee was skeptical of the Jug. He'd preferred to stay with the group's beloved Spitfires. Before the mission, one of the other pilots in his squadron tried to cheer him up. "Look at it this way," he told the frustrated flyer, "they'll never be able to dive away from us again." This was a textbook example: the 190s were used to outrunning Spitfires by pointing their noses downward. They instinctively headed for the deck when the P-47s pounced.

The Jugs steadily drew closer to the German fighters. At five hundred feet, Blakeslee exploded his victim with a heavy-hitting burst from his battery of .50-calibers. Two other Jug flyers got victories that day, but three Thunderbolts failed to return. When Blakeslee's squadron mates were congratulating him, one told him, "You see, I told you the Jug could out-dive them!" The major spat back, "Well it damn well ought to be able to dive—it sure as hell can't climb!"

More fighter sweeps followed, but the Germans were only mildly interested in a fight. They had learned to save their energy for the bombers. There was little sense in tangling with the Thunderbolts alone. The exception came on April 29, when the three groups fielded three squadrons of twelve Thunderbolts each. Skilled German fighter pilots bushwhacked two squadrons of the 56th near Woensdretch, Holland. Two Americans and their aircraft were lost while several Thunderbolts returned despite serious damage. The Americans claimed no enemy aircraft in the one-sided brawl.

ESCORT

Thunderbolt units initially focused on escorting bombers: "Ramrod missions," as they were called. The Thunderbolt could fly farther than the short-ranged Spitfires, but not by much. Most of Germany remained beyond the Thunderbolts at this early stage.

Antwerp, Belgium, was another story. On May 4,

One of the last Evansville-built razorback P-47Ds pulls alongside a B-17 Flying Fortress during a return trip to England. The bare-metal Jug carries the black-and-white checkered cowling of the 78th Fighter Group. *National Archives*

Nothing looks as good to the bomber crews as an escort of what they called "Little Friends." But often, American fighter pilots were a bit more cautious during these aerial meetings, preferring to keep a safe distance. Jug drivers claimed that the flyers in the bombers would shoot at anything that came near. When cruising into range, Thunderbolt pilots did it slowly; it was best not to surprise anyone. *National Archives*

1943, B-17 bombers struck the Ford truck factory there. For the first time, all three Thunderbolt groups, along with other Allied fighters, escorted the bombers.

Range always defined escort work. No fighters could stay with the bombers through the whole mission. The escorts flew in relays, some covering the attack, some covering the withdrawal. The 78th flew with a diversionary force toward Paris.

The higher speed required by the Thunderbolts to stay effective diminished the time that the planes could cover the bombers. While the speed of a Flying Fortress was around 150 miles per hour, P-47s flew at 240 or more. The fighters would zigzag back and forth several thousand feet above the bomber formations,

waiting to roar down on any German threat that came up to meet them.

The net result was that the already fuel-pinched Jugs had to fly a few miles for every straight-line mile of coverage. Typical time over the bombers amounted to thirty minutes. Frequently, the frustrated bomber crewman noted, there were no nearby Allied fighters at all. And, P-47 coverage could only reach two hundred miles from the Thunderbolt's home airfield.

Observing these time and distance voids in the protection scheme, the German Luftwaffe learned to take advantage of the gaps. However, for the Antwerp attack, things went relatively well. The 4th Fighter Group lost a plane and pilot due to engine failure, but they also shot down an Fw-190.

The 56th pilots thought they'd gotten a Messerschmitt Bf-109 during the withdrawal, but it turned out they had attacked an RAF Spitfire, which, of course, soured everyone's mood. At least the B-17s had hit the Ford factory, completing their job without a loss.

As the weeks progressed, it was hard times for the "Jugheads." The damage they were able to inflict on the Germans was less than their losses. Especially troubling were mechanical difficulties: missing planes and dead pilots due to engine failures. Fixing the Thunderbolt's reactions to the cold, humid air over Europe was a priority.

Interestingly, the 56th Fighter Group, the most steadfast supporter of the P-47, had yet to claim a victory. The ten German fighters conclusively shot down in the first two months went to 4th and 78th pilots. The 56th

The plane in the foreground was the fighter flown by Maj. Horace "Pappy" Craig. The Thunderbolt farther away from the camera was Capt. Eugene O'Neill's aircraft, which survived the war and, amazingly, found its way to the Far East to be used in transition training. Both aircraft were in service with the 56th Fighter Group at the time this image was taken. *The Museum of Flight, American Fighter Aces Association*

had lost three planes but had nothing to show for it.

To better influence the air battles, the Jugs needed to increase their combat radius by carrying more fuel. The first P-47s used big, bulbous two-hundred-gallon ferry tanks, affixed to their bellies. Unpressurized, they could only be used at low altitudes. In addition, they were an aerodynamic nightmare. However, they *could* be carried half full, used during the long climb over the English Channel, and then dropped. This unwieldy process added seventy-five miles of radius.

More elegant, teardrop-shaped 75-gallon metal tanks, and 108-gallon pressed paper tanks were on the way. They were pressurized units that affected the Jug's flight qualities less significantly. Pilots called them "babies." Carrying a center-point drop tank on the outbound leg of an escort mission allowed the aircraft to reach 325 miles.

When Thunderbolts, lugging their babies, started appearing at distances the Germans had dismissed as impossible, the hunting improved. Captain Charles London of the 78th Fighter Group became the first P-47 ace, bringing his personal score to five on June 29. He shot down two Bf-109s positioning themselves to attack American bombers.

But the German fighter pilots were veterans, still able to prey on those new to the air-fighting game. A few days before London's milestone action, the hard-luck 56th Fighter Group encountered Focke-Wulfs as they were covering the bombers' withdrawal from Villacoublay, France.

A mass of German fighters jumped the 56th from behind. Airplanes scattered all over the skies. Lieutenant Robert Johnson's P-47 was hit in the opening melee with cannon and machine gun fire, his burning Thunderbolt

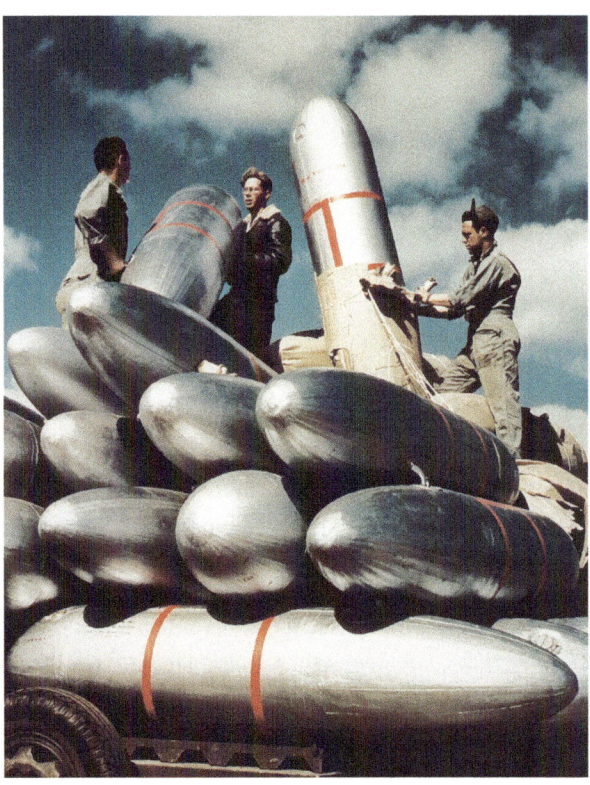

Used by P-47 fighters to extend their range, British-made 108-gallon tanks were created from glue-impregnated paper, which could hold fuel long enough to do the job. Later versions of the tanks were made of metal and painted gray instead of the silver coating used on the "paper babies." *National Archives*

tumbling earthward. His first instinct was to get out, but the canopy slid back only six inches and jammed.

With no other choice, Johnson regained control of his crippled plane and pointed the nose west. Against all odds, the ravaged plane flew on, blasted and smoking. Johnson himself was burned, doused in the eyes with

A flight of 56th Fighter Group Jugs cruises the skies over Europe looking for trouble. This image was reported to have belonged to famous Thunderbolt ace Robert Johnson. *The Museum of Flight, American Fighter Aces Association*

The shredded area behind Lt. Robert Johnson's canopy on his P-47C, *All Hell*, was what started a series of events that almost cost him his life. Unable to bail out, there was nothing he could do as a German fighter peppered his ship with bullets. Note the broken side window—the only way to remove him from the cockpit once he landed. *The Museum of Flight, American Fighter Aces Association*

Ace Robert Johnson, of the 56th Fighter Group, and his crew chief before a mission. By the end of the war, he would claim twenty-eight aircraft, but many studies only give him credit for twenty-seven. *National Archives*

stinging hydraulic fluid, wounded by shrapnel and bullets, and suffering from oxygen deprivation. It didn't take long for his flying junk heap to attract the attention of a German hunter, moving in for an easy kill.

Johnson could do nothing as the blue-speckled Focke-Wulf leisurely cruised up behind his flying wreck. He could only make a feeble attempt to protect himself by pulling his arms in close to his body and dropping his seat down to gain the full protection of the armor plate behind the cockpit. The German fighter fired.

In his classic book, *Thunderbolt*, Johnson describes the terrible feeling: "I don't move an inch. I sit, anger building up. The bullets tear metal, rip into spars, grinding away, chopping up the Thunderbolt. My nerves grate as if both hands hold a charge of electricity. Sharp jolts against my back. Less than an inch away, bullets crash against the armor."

And yet the venerable Jug inexplicably continued to fly. After each series of bursts, the German pilot pulled alongside Johnson's battered plane, not quite believing that the Thunderbolt was still in the air. Luckily for Johnson, the 190 pilot had used all of his cannon ammunition before he'd encountered such a juicy target—if collecting a whole load of 7.92mm bullets in your hide can be called lucky!

After absorbing every bullet the Fw-190's pilot had

on board, the engine in Johnson's plane kept running, the propeller eating up the miles toward the English Channel, dragging the sieved airframe and its exhausted pilot behind. The German pulled alongside one last time and observed his handiwork for several minutes before he peeled into a climbing turn toward his own home airfield.

Miraculously, Johnson's blasted Thunderbolt, named *All Hell*, brought him home. There were twenty-one gaping holes made by 20mm cannon shells and hundreds of holes from 7.92mm guns. While Johnson went to the hospital, his beloved plane went to the scrap pile, never to fly again. Others were less fortunate. While the 56th claimed two victories, the group lost four pilots and five planes. Another four made it home with extensive damage.

Thunderbolts were tough. There was little doubt about that. Lieutenant Dean Morehouse dove low, evading antiaircraft fire. He plowed through a row of fifty-foot trees and came back to England, his fighter covered in branches and foliage. Lieutenant Arlo Henry went him one better. Scooting away from a flak tower over a farmer's field, he flew as low as he dared. Back at base, his crew chief was startled to find turnips in the plane's air scoop, churned up by the propeller.

COMPRESSIBILITY

It was well known that the P-47 could "drop like a bag of bricks." In stateside flight tests, P-47s were lost after entering dives from high altitudes; examination of the wreckage revealed the tail structure had failed. Designers immediately strengthened the aircraft. Later crashes showed that the fabric-covered tail surfaces had torn free, leading Republic to switch to metal-covered elevators and rudder. Strengthening the tail gave the Thunderbolt and its pilot a good chance to survive a "death dive."

When Maj. Cass Hough dove the P-47 during testing in England, he reported attaining a speed of 780 miles per hour. Over Germany, Lt. Robert Knapp said he found his throttle and control surfaces frozen while tangling with Nazi fighters. He dropped from twenty-eight thousand feet to five thousand before wrenching the stick back, pulling out, and running for home. Incredibly, he claimed to have hit 850 miles per hour!

Engineers and designers at Republic were, of course, suspicious of these claims. No propeller-driven aircraft could ever fly beyond the speed of sound. But to the pilots trapped in the hurtling mass of metal, it may

This P-47C 5-RE was flown by Capt. Eugene O'Neill of the 56th Fighter Group and carried an image of Li'l Abner on its cowling. *National Archives*

Model:	P-47C-5-RE
Number Built:	362
Engine:	Pratt & Whitney R-2800-21
Power Rating:	2,000 hp
Propeller:	Curtiss Electric, 12 feet 2 inches diameter
Span:	40 feet 9.56 inches
Length:	36 feet 1.19 inches
Height:	14 feet 3.56 inches
Wing Area:	300 square feet
Empty Weight:	9,900 pounds
Gross Weight:	13,500 pounds
Maximum Weight:	14,925 pounds
Maximum Speed:	420 mph at 30,000 feet
Landing Speed:	104 mph
Service Ceiling:	42,000 feet
Internal Fuel:	305 gallons
Maximum Range:	835 miles at 10,000 feet
Armament:	8 x .50-caliber machine guns, 300 to 425 rounds per gun

have seemed that way. The Thunderbolt's amazingly strong airframe, combined with its weight and incredible speed in an all-out dive from high altitude, created factors that led to a phenomenon aerodynamicists

Early on, Thunderbolt pilots found that their Jugs could take punishment as well as they could dish it out. Lieutenant Justus Foster returned to England with solid hits from five 20mm shells in the hide of his P-47. The blown tire and bent propeller were from his hard landing back at base. If it hadn't been for the Thunderbolt's amazingly stout construction, the plane most likely wouldn't have made it back. *National Archives*

called "compressibility."

As the Thunderbolt dropped at near the speed of sound, the air passing over the plummeting fighter would accelerate even more. Instead of smoothly flowing over the wing as during normal flight, the air was violently displaced by the onrushing plane.

This compressibility shock—supersonic shockwaves moving over the aircraft—created voids over the plane's control surfaces, rendering them useless. Severe buffeting took place, jerking the stick violently. Suddenly, the buffeting stopped and the stick became rigid. Pilots related that the stick felt like it was "stuck in concrete." It made for one terrifying ride for the flyer in the cockpit. And as if the pilot weren't scared enough, the wing's center of lift moved aft several feet, making the Thunderbolt menacingly nose-heavy once it entered the compressibility zone. This steepened the dive. (Alexander Kartveli discussed another strange phenomenon with a *Life* magazine reporter. His pilots told him that during high-speed dives the blast tubes over the machine gun barrels in the wings suddenly turned vibrant blue.)

Struggling to pull out, pilots attempted a variety of methods to recover. One of the worst was rolling the elevator trim to the stops. As the plane descended into lower, thicker air, and the plane left the compressibility range, the trim tabs "took hold," usually in about two or three second's time.

The correct response was to ride out the dive, add

This P-47D Thunderbolt, *Little Chief*, was flown by ace Lt. Frank Klibbe, who is credited with seven victories during his service with the 56th Fighter Group. *The Museum of Flight, Champlin collection*

some power, and begin to apply back pressure to the stick. At around eighteen thousand feet, the experts told the pilots, they would begin to regain control. The pilot had instructions to begin pulling the stick back firmly: too much, and the stress would break the plane apart; too little, and the ground would do even worse.

A paper released by Republic insisted that a pilot should never get into a near-vertical dive: "[the maneuver is] of no tactical significance, requires a lengthy recovery period, and results in a loss of initiative in combat." But in combat, flyers learned quickly that they might try all sorts of things, including a straight-down dive, if it meant escape from a lead-spitting Bf-109. In combat, anything and everything happened. They probably chuckled as they read through the paper. It included helpful thoughts like, "If the recovery is too gentle, the tremendous loss of altitude during recovery may be fatal." They were all familiar with what that meant!

ON THE WARPATH

Even with the Thunderbolt's quirks, pilots were growing fond of their new mounts. With fuel capacity increased, the P-47s forced the Luftwaffe's air assets to gradually move eastward to protect their homeland. For a time, the Germans tried to rise up to meet the incoming P-47s near the English Channel, forcing them to drop their extra fuel and engage in combat. This tactic prevented the P-47s from rendezvousing with the bombers, due to lack of fuel. The Jug pilots made the Germans pay dearly

The German Messerschmitt Bf-109 gets a heavy dose of lead from American .50-caliber guns. Fighter pilots said the best way to dispatch a foe was to come in from behind, incredibly close, so that there was very little chance to miss. *National Archives*

Taking off one at a time wasted precious gasoline. Here, Thunderbolts launch in pairs. If the field would allow it, the fighters would even take off in fours or more. Here, the planes carry the never-very-popular 150-gallon flat-section paper fuel tanks. *National Museum of the United States Air Force*

for the attacks, piling in and knocking the enemy planes out of the fight. The scores of many P-47 pilots rose as they learned how to slash the once seemingly unstoppable Focke-Wulfs and Messerschmitts.

These early interceptions proved disastrous for the Germans. They could usually only commit a small number to the attacks, and those that challenged the Thunderbolts to drop their babies often got thumped. As more Allied fighters were committed to Eighth Air Force units, a squadron or two would take care of the Germans, while others, expendable fuel tanks still affixed, would cruise onward undisturbed.

To be most effective, the Nazi fighter units were forced to wait until the American fighters were low on fuel and turned toward home. The Luftwaffe became experts at it. One U.S. combat report tells the story. When asked to pinpoint the "place where attacked," a bomber crewman instead described an event. You can almost sense his exasperation as he hammers on his typewriter: "Just after the P-47s left."

The balance of power, however, was changing. More Allied machines rumbled over targets with each passing week. By November 1943, the once snake-bitten 56th Fighter Group had surged ahead of the pack, downing a total of one hundred Nazi planes. The total victory-versus-loss ratio for all Thunderbolt units stood at 237 to 73.

German aircraft and pilots were caught in a downward spiral. There were plenty of operational losses—hundreds of casualties while attacking the American bomber streams and then tangling with American fighters. The fights with the barrel-nosed Thunderbolts hurt the most, but then there were also the fork-tailed P-38 Lightnings, which could fly even farther into the skies over the Fatherland. And there were reports of a new plane, a Merlin-powered machine called Mustang.

The Mustang was rumored to be stingy enough on fuel to stay with the bomber for hours. The P-51 could fly beyond Berlin and back.

As they awaited the arrival of this miracle plane in large numbers, the Jugheads trudged on. The old orders of "stick with the bombers, no matter what" changed to "engage any German aircraft you see, chase them down, and kill them off." Fighter pilots, naturally, were big fans of the latter.

The orders went beyond attacking Nazi planes in the air. After their escort duties were over, Thunderbolt pilots used up the rest of their fuel while hunting at low level, blasting any targets they could find, including enemy planes parked on the ground. Dropping to nearly zero altitude would have been difficult for earlier model P-47s, but now water injection combined with new paddle-blade propellers made the heavy fighter a factor below fifteen thousand feet as well as above.

Attacks on airfields were touchy affairs. The Germans usually had them well covered with antiaircraft guns. One key was speed, as Capt. Gordon Compton of the 353rd Fighter Group related. Attacks should be "carried out in a 'balls out,' aggressive manner" at more than three hundred miles per hour. The Thunderbolts would dive, come in low, up sun and line abreast, then rise up to one hundred feet at the airfield's perimeter to pick out targets. Each flyer would fly straight at his chosen objective—a hangar, parked aircraft, or gun position—and hammer it with a long, concentrated burst of .50-calibers. Then the P-47s would continue on, as low as they dared, departing the area and climbing away a mile or so later. Many flyers related that more than one pass was considered very risky.

Everyone had their modifications to the plan and various tips of advice for fellow pilots: "If your target is a gun emplacement, start firing early to scare them." "Approach into the wind. It makes you hard to hear until

Continued on page 66

Colonel David Schilling of the 56th Fighter Group poses near the red snout of his Thunderbolt. The 56th, upon seeing the brightly colored German fighters they were encountering over Europe, decided to paint over their white cowl rings with red. The pilots figured, as they dove on the enemy, it might give the Nazi pilot just a split second of indecision—friend or foe. *National Archives*

COL. STEVE PISANOS—FLYING P-47s IN THE 4TH FIGHTER GROUP

Retired Col. Steve N. Pisanos was born in Athens, Greece, and came to America in 1938. He flew P-51s and Spitfires with the Royal Air Force before the United States entered World War II. He became an ace while piloting a P-47 with the 4th Fighter Group. Pisanos discussed the Thunderbolt in an interview with the author.

I understand the 4th Fighter Group was a bit reluctant to transfer over to the P-47 Thunderbolt after flying the Spitfire in combat. What would you say was the general consensus and mood of your comrades about the switch?

When it was announced that the 4th Fighter Group was going to be re-equipped with the P-47 Thunderbolt, some pilots at Debden Aerodrome felt that maybe we made a mistake leaving the Royal Air Force. But as the days went by, we began to think about the pay in Uncle Sam's air force, which was mighty good.

And when the P-47s began to arrive and we started to fly the clumsy seven-ton monster, the negative attitude many of us had formed about the Jug began to disappear. Even though the P-47 was twice as heavy as the Spit, and it couldn't turn or climb as well as the Spit, it could out dive any German or British fighter. It could also fly farther than the Spit.

After we had completed our training (twenty-five to thirty flying hours per pilot to become operational), we had surprisingly discovered that the seven-ton battlewagon of war could fight well against Germany's fighters at high altitudes, because of the highly effective turbo supercharger. We also learned that we could bounce anything below from our high altitude and get away by zooming up to infinity. We learned to avoid getting mixed up with the German fighters below eighteen thousand feet.

On April 15, 1943, Major Don Blakeslee of the 4th Fighter Group shot down a Fw-190 during a fighter sweep across the Channel, the first enemy aircraft to be shot down by a P-47 Thunderbolt. We hated to see our beloved Spitfires go, but we had now fallen in love with another fighter aircraft, the P-47, which could take us deeper into enemy territory.

Before Spitfires, you had flown P-51As in England. Do you suppose your experiences with an American plane made your outlook on what to expect from the Thunderbolt any different than that of your squadron mates?

In a way, yes. The P-51A wasn't a high-altitude fighter. Its Allison engine had no supercharger, and above ten thousand feet the aircraft became sluggish. That is why the RAF used it for low-level operations over Holland.

But I was certainly impressed with the cockpit arrangement of the American machine of war, in comparison to the Spitfire's cockpit. When I first got into the cockpit of the Thunderbolt to familiarize myself with the many gadgets, I certainly felt like I was at home.

Did the pilots of the 4th Fighter Group discuss how they were going to change their tactics to accommodate the very different type of fighter?

During training, all of us were involved in mock dogfights, among ourselves and frequently getting mixed up with friendly Spitfires, Typhoons, and Hurricanes. We used mostly our bounce technique, dive and zoom up. This type of involvement gave us not only confidence, but we learned what to expect when we were to be confronted with Luftwaffe fighters.

Also, every night before dinner at the bar and after, still drinking, there was talk such as how to attack Jerry from above, or get away from one you had spotted on your tail, and how to recover from a dive. Recovering from a dive was very important to us because during training, we had a pilot who went into almost a vertical dive and crashed straight in. Although investigators couldn't find a reason for the crash, it was assumed that the pilot had perhaps blacked out in his attempt to recover.

As for myself, I did considerable dogfighting, tail chasing, and everything you could expect in a mix-up with an adversary. I accomplished most of this

Steve Pisanos not only flew his Thuderbolt, *Miss Plainfield*, in combat, he also piloted Mustangs and Spitfires. When forced to crash-land in enemy territory in 1944 (while flying a Mustang), he spent six months evading the Germans and fighting with the French Resistance and American Office of Strategic Services (OSS). *The Museum of Flight, American Fighter Aces collection*

part of our training with my roommate, Don Gentile. We would take off and rendezvous at a pre-arranged place, climb to altitude in formation, then break up and try and get on each other's tail. This, to me and to my close friend, was the most valuable part of our training with the Jug.

I understand that you became a U.S. citizen while you were in the USAAF, flying in England. Your P-47 was named *Miss Plainfield*. This is for your adopted home in the United States?

Yes, Plainfield, New Jersey, was my adopted town in the U.S. That was the place I worked and lived and the place from where I joined the RAF in the latter part of 1941.

When I was assigned my own P-47 (QP-D), my crew chief, Sgt. Paul Fox, said to me one day, "Lieutenant, aren't we going to paint something on the cowling of our Jug? Your friend has already painted *Miss Dallas* on his Jug and it looks real good."

I decided to name my P-47 *Miss Plainfield* for a girl from that city, who had started to send me letters, praising me for being in the war from Plainfield, as the local newspaper continued to write articles about my activities while I was overseas. I never met this young lady.

Tell me about your first combat mission in the P-47.

On May 21, 1943, the 4th Fighter Group was dispatched on a fighter sweep over Belgium. I was

Pisanos' P-47-D Thunderbolt, QP-D, of the 4th Fighter Group, 344th Fighter Squadron, in Debden, England. *The Museum of Flight, American Fighter Aces collection*

wingman to Capt. Tommy Andrews of White Section. Just as we crossed the enemy coast at thirty-one thousand feet, Corby Control advised us about some twelve bandits approaching from nine o'clock, angels twenty-seven.

Upon sighting them, Captain Andrews immediately broke away from group formation, turned left, and went into a shallow dive. The Germans broke up formation, and the twelve or so Fw-190s scattered all over the sky. Tommy cut onto the radio and said, "White Section, two 190s, twelve o'clock below, let's go get them."

As we were closing in fast on the two Germans from behind and a little bit above, they broke up their element, turning in opposite directions. On Tommy's orders, [Gordon] Whitlow and [Leland] "Mack" [Mac-Farlane] followed the guy to the right, and Tommy said, "Follow me Spiro (using my Greek name). We'll go after the guy on the left."

Both of us were barreling down at high speed, but as Tommy got within range of his prey, the German snapped his aircraft to the left in a very steep turn, forcing Tommy to overshoot the 190 by a big margin. The German must have been a clever guy, I thought.

Having gone by the 190, Tommy made an extremely steep left turn that scared the heck out of me, forcing me to pull up in a sort of left wingover, with my eyes still glued on the 190 that had passed under my aircraft.

Tommy's turn was so steep that he must have experienced a high-speed stall, as his aircraft flipped over on its back and went into what appeared to be a flat spin. "Tommy," I screamed into the radio, "are you okay?" "I'm okay," he said and added, "Dammit, I screwed up. Go get that bastard, Spiro, and I'll catch up with you."

Immediately, I took my eyes away from Tommy's Jug and turned around toward the fleeing 190. I put my aircraft into a dive with full power, and that helped me catch up with the guy. I must have been about four hundred yards out when the German evidently spotted me as he started to turn left—my favorite turn with the Jug.

I tightened my turn as he did his, but I was able to slide inside his turn, and that put me some 250 to 300 yards behind him in a perfect position for a deflection shot. I pressed the trigger and gave him a short burst, remembering my old friend Deacon Hively. You start with a short burst to make sure you are getting hits, as you don't want to waste any ammo. But dammit, every one of my bullets from the eight .50s went to the right of the steeply turning 190.

I tightened my turn some more and fired again—a long burst and bang, black smoke began to pour from the 190. The smoke was getting heavier, and suddenly the German aircraft stopped turning, and I had him now in the center of my gun sight. I gave him another burst, and still the only thing I saw was more black smoke and no fire of any kind.

"Atta boy, you nailed him," Tommy Andrews said on the radio. He had caught up with me after his ordeal. "I am behind you White Two, go on and finish the bastard." The 190 slowed, and I had to cut my speed and pull up to the right to get out of the heavy smoke. I looked at the 190 and the cockpit was totally covered in smoke, and I couldn't see the pilot.

"Why on earth was the pilot not jumping?" I asked myself. Then all of a sudden the canopy blew off, and I thought the pilot was going to jump, but nothing happened. "He must have been injured," I thought.

It was then that I decided to turn away and go home, as I had spent considerable time in the area. Tommy must have been thinking the same thing, as he cut into the radio and said, "Let's turn around Spiro, the guy is done. He has to jump now."

Since I had not seen the pilot jump or the plane crash, I could only claim one Fw-190 *probably* destroyed, based on the rules of combat. Later, Fighter Command upgraded the claim to one Fw-190 destroyed, based on a report of a pilot who saw two parachutes floating in the area of operation—one a P-47 pilot and the other from my Fw-190.

Was the P-47 well suited for the type of work done in the Eighth Air Force, bomber escort business?

The Thunderbolt was the most suitable aircraft for escort duty at the time, even though it wasn't the ideal aircraft for individual combat at low altitudes unless the adversary you were after happened to be an inexperienced pilot.

At high altitude, however, the Jug was as good as or better than the 109 or the 190, and this was the way we used to fly escort missions with the B-17s and B-24s: We would position one squadron at least a few thousand feet above the bomber formation, and if any enemy aircraft attempted to attack the bombers, we would merely dive with the intention of cutting them off and maneuver, using our speed for an advantageous position to fire our guns.

Some attacking Germans would dive away. Others would stay around to fight. Of course, those who had elected to dive were asking for trouble, because they could never out-dive the Jug.

How did the 4th Fighter Group take to losing their P-47s? Where you sorry to see them go?

Don Blakeslee, who commanded the 4th Fighter Group, insisted all along that his pilots be given a fighter that could provide escort all the way to targets deep inside Germany. In fact, when he saw the P-51B groups arriving in England, and 8th Fighter Command used him a few times to lead these groups into combat, he realized that the Mustang was the answer to long-distance escort.

He begged Gen. Bill Kepner, the chief of the 8th Fighter Command, to give the 4th Fighter Group the Mustang, and the general's reply was that he couldn't take the 4th off operations for the transition to train pilots. Blakeslee countered the general's remark by saying, "General, we don't need any training, we flew Spitfires. You give me the Mustangs and I'll be ready to go in twenty-four hours."

It worked. A few days later, Kepner called and asked, "Don, is that twenty-four hours you had told me about, is it still on?"

"Yes, sir," Blakeslee told him. On February 28 [1944], the 4th flew its first mission with Mustangs. We were out on the 29th and on March 2. But on March 3, we made history by escorting the B-17s to Berlin the first time.

As to whether the 4th Fighter Group pilots were sorry to see our faithful P-47s go, it's hard to tell. Some pilots loved the machine because of its ruggedness. But Don Blakeslee, our industrious leader, had other ideas. He wanted to go to Berlin, and the Thunderbolt was not suitable for the accomplishment of that mission. Going to Berlin with the Mustang was the ultimate warning to the Luftwaffe that the USAAF meant business now.

Continued from page 61

"Approach into the wind. It makes you hard to hear until you're right on top of the target." "Remember, the closer to the guns you fly, the harder it is for them to get you."

Advances were being made in the escort game too. New wing-mounted gas tanks and the necessary plumbing allowed the P-47s to carry two 108-gallon tanks, increasing their radius to 475 miles. This change came just in time for U.S. bombing attacks that later would be dubbed "the Big Week."

German aircraft manufacturing and assembly plants were often the targets on the heavily escorted missions to Leipzig, Brunswick, Gotha, Regensburg, Schweinfurt, Augsburg, Stuttgart, and Steyr. Not only were the attacks meant to damage the aviation industry on the ground, American flyers deliberately forced Luftwaffe units into fights in the air in order to destroy their combat effectiveness. Bomber gunners and fighters claimed more than six hundred Nazi fighters shot down.

With more resources available all the time, limited numbers of long-range P-51s and P-38s worked along much of the route, with masses of Thunderbolts covering the areas in the path where German fighters were most likely to be encountered. A breakdown of seven

major attacks into Germany from early 1944 shows how the three types of fighters fared:

	P-47	P-38	P-51
Total No. of Sorties	3,846	518	470
Total Claims*	199-20-100	25-5-15	83-7-56
Victories per 1,000 Sorties	52.4	48.2	176.6
Aircraft Lost to Enemy Aircraft	25	17	14
Aircraft Lost per 1,000 Sorties	6.5	32.8	29.7
Ratio of Victories to Combat Losses	8:1	1.5:1	6:1
Pilots Killed or Missing	23	17	13
Pilots Lost per 1,000 Sorties	5.98	32.82	27.66

* Claims in this order: destroyed, probably destroyed, and damaged

The sheer number of Thunderbolts available was staggering. On February 25, 1944, there were 139 P-51s and 73 P-38s escorting the streams of bombers headed for Messerschmitt aircraft factories in three cities. Along with them were 687 Republic P-47s! And when trouble came, Jug pilots would switch to internal fuel, waggle their auxiliary tanks loose, flip the gun safety off, and turn their gun sight on. It was show time.

Captain Duane Beeson of the 4th Fighter Group came out of his dive at nearly five hundred miles per hour, spooking two pilots in Focke-Wulfs who were harassing a lonely, crippled bomber. His first shots missed, but with so much speed, he was able to zoom back up, turn, and drop again as the Nazi planes turned tail in different directions.

The pilot the other flyers called "Bee" was described as "a diminutive fellow with big hands and wrists, [like

A Thunderbolt and what is reported to be a Nazi fighter mix it up over Emden, Germany. The Jug pilot doesn't look like he has complete control of the situation, but luckily for him, help is on the way. The grainy image was taken from the gun camera of another P-47 diving into the fight. *National Archives*

The camouflaged P-47M flown by Maj. Michael Jackson of the 56th Fighter Group at Boxted, England. *Teddy* carries eight black crosses, indicating air victories, and six white crosses, for aircraft destroyed on the ground. *Stan Piet*

a] boy not quite grown." He was known as an aggressive pilot who, strangely, flew with both hands on the stick, left thumb over the button for the .50-calibers. But he held his fire as the propeller of his Thunderbolt chopped the air, closing the distance between him and his prey. When the fleeing fighter filled his gun sight, his thumb jammed down, and armor-piercing incendiary (API) rounds sparkled and flashed over his victim. Fractions of a second later, Beeson's Thunderbolt zoomed ahead of the slowing Focke-Wulf. It was a veteran maneuver: "Never slow down to watch your victim," pilots said, "or you just might become a victim yourself." Beeson's wingman saw the German plane smash into the ground.

CHANGING OF THE GUARD

After the Big Week, it was on to missions over Germany's capital, Berlin, in early March. By this time, many units in the Eighth Air Force, including the 4th Fighter Group, were beginning to switch to the P-51 Mustang. The changeover would take time, and many a bomber crewman anxiously scanning the skies would continue to see the great formations of P-47s throughout 1944. The flyers called their escorts "Little Friends," though neither the P-47, nor the P-51 for that matter, were all that little.

How strange that the Mustang, originally used by the U.S. Army as a ground-attack aircraft, would excel at long-range escort. Equally puzzling was the fact that the Thunderbolt, built as a high-altitude interceptor, would soon find a new niche nearer to the ground than its speedy, high-flying cousin.

Over time, the 56th Fighter Group was the only Eighth Air Force fighter outfit to resist the change to the P-51. Instead, they eventually took command of newer, more powerful P-47M models. The 56th, operating only Thunderbolts, would become the highest-scoring unit of the Eighth Air Force, with 674 planes shot down, and would produce Europe's two top aces, Francis "Gabby" Gabreski (twenty-eight kills) and Robert Johnson (twenty-seven).

But in the first months of 1944, the war was far from over. American pilots would continue to fight, seeking out targets in the air and on the ground. As plans were being made for the invasion of France and eventual push into Germany, bombers and their escorts continued to brave the terrible weather in England and rumble over their targets with regularity and in ever-growing numbers. But by this time, some of the less humble Thunderbolt pilots said, the Luftwaffe was all but dead.

Sighting-in the guns and rocket tubes of a 57th Fighter Group Thunderbolt, ground crews have raised the tail of the fighter to flying attitude and carefully screened the air scoop to keep it from sucking up dirt and rocks. *National Archives*

Lieutenant George Novotny (center) stands with some of the men who keep his P-47D, *Lady Janie VI/Ruthless Ruthie*, flying with the 325th Fighter Group. Note the open breeches on the Thunderbolt's guns and the big 165-gallon, P-38-type drop tanks under the wings. *The Museum of Flight, Champlin collection*

CHAPTER FIVE
THE WAR TO THE SOUTH: P-47s IN THE MEDITERRANEAN

There was more than one path into Germany. The men who fought in North Africa and northward into Europe are often forgotten in the history books. Flyers equipped with outdated fighter aircraft—P-38s, P-39s, and P-40s—helped forcibly remove the Germans and Italians from North Africa in late 1942 and 1943 before P-47s were ever delivered. The "Jugheads" flying from Italy pioneered many of the weapons and tactics used later in the fighting over Western Europe.

THE CHECKERTAILS

The first unit on the Mediterranean to receive Thunderbolts was the 325th Fighter Group, known as the "Checkertail Clan." Their battered and sand-blasted Curtiss P-40s carried distinct yellow and black diagonally oriented checkered tails.

Pilots glumly observed that flying Curtiss P-40s, you couldn't outrun a Messerschmitt and you couldn't outclimb one either. To make it home, you had to fight—and you had to win.

By late 1943, the 325th exchanged its Warhawks for new Thunderbolts. The unit moved north to Foggia Main airfield in Italy. The army sent Republic representatives and veteran pilots from P-47 outfits in England to help the Checkertails with the transition to the longer-range and higher-flying Jug.

Their missions emphasized escorting heavy and medium bombers while occasionally conducting ground-attack sorties. The Clan's first combat mission with Jugs took place December 14, 1943, when they shepherded bombers to targets in Greece. During the first month, rough weather threatened more than the enemy. The low point came on Christmas Day, when the 325th lost three Thunderbolts and pilots when they plowed into a mountainside hidden in pea-soup clouds.

A high point came more than a month later when the 325th Fighter Group's commander, Lt. Col. Robert Baseler, led his men on a surprise attack on January 30, 1944. The enemy air forces, it seemed, nearly always attacked the American heavy-bomber formations as they neared their target. The Clan this time slipped into the Villaorba area at low level over the Adriatic Sea, trying to catch the German fighters as they prepared for the "main event."

With Baseler's Thunderbolt, named *Big Stud*, in the

Lieutenant Charles King sits on his "Checkertail Clan" Thunderbolt. The one-foot squares made for easy recognition. *The Museum of Flight, Champlin collection*

lead, the group set off, so close to the deck that pilots claimed their prop tips made wakes in the water as they "motor-boated" more than three hundred miles. It was during the trip that the flyers discovered something terrifying about a tiny detail of the P-47's cockpit. Some engineer in Farmingdale had decided to locate the fuel selector switch on the cockpit floor. Though Baseler may not have noticed (his pilots joked he had eight-foot arms), it was quite a trick to bend down by the left side of the seat to switch from the depleted wing tanks to internal fuel. A slight pull back on the stick could wreck the element of surprise for the mission. And a hair of downward pressure for that critical second or two would spell a fate much worse than that.

But the flight went on undetected and unharmed, arriving over the enemy airfields not only as the German defending elements readied for battle, but also as other Axis aircraft were being ferried out of the danger zone. There were Messerschmitt, Focke-Wulf, and Macchi fighters as well as retreating German bombers, transports, and scout aircraft all over the sky as the 325th Jugs roared into the mix.

Captain Herschel "Herky" Green and others tore into a line of Junkers Ju-52 cargo planes, the P-47 pilots pushing each other out the way to participate in the

"turkey shoot." Herky claims he executed a 180-degree turn after a pass, only to find smoking splotches in the sky where the German planes had once been only seconds before. No matter, there were other targets close at hand. Besides the four Ju-52s he blasted, Green also shot down a Macchi M.C. 202 and exploded a twin-engine Dornier Do-217.

During the massive air battle, the American bombers arrived, unmolested, and dropped their bombs on the airfields from high above. Major Lewis "Bill" Chick saw the Bf-109 he was chasing suddenly pull out of its weaving maneuvers, fly straight and level, and "pour on the coals." Chick instinctively looked around to see what he was missing. Overhead, he was gazing into the emptying bomb bays of a fleet of American B-17s. Chick jokes that he nearly passed his quarry as he tried to scurry out of a patch of sky rapidly filling with hundreds of fragmentation bombs. After they were clear, he latched back on the Messerschmitt's tail and finished the job.

Losing only two of their own, the 325th bagged thirty-eight planes before the day was over. They flew Thunderbolts until May 1944, when the group switched to P-51 Mustangs. During its time as a P-47 unit, the 325th flew over 3,600 sorties, shooting down 153 enemy aircraft while losing 38 aircraft of their own. Interestingly, the Thunderbolts of the 325th were transferred directly to another famous group within the Mediterranean Theater of Operations (MTO). The new owners, the 332nd Fighter Group, painted the checkered tails of

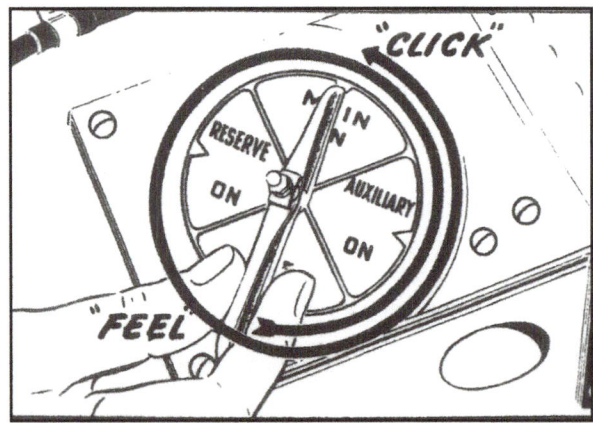

A drawing of the dreaded fuel selector switch, taken from a P-47 pilot's manual. When flying at low altitude over the water, it took some skill or a lot of luck to find the correct setting without plowing into the waves. *Cradle of Aviation Museum*

the well-worn Thunderbolts all red. The flyers and personnel of the group were made up completely of African-American men—Tuskegee Airmen.

THE TUSKEGEE AIRMEN

They took to flying the planes almost immediately, even before army and Republic representatives arrived to show them how. One crew chief recalls sitting at the field, listening to a tech rep tell them that the heavy Jug should never be slow-rolled under one thousand feet. No sooner were the words out of his mouth than a pair of Thunderbolts returned from a successful mission. Lieutenants Pruitt and Archer wrenched their fighters into a victory roll, in formation, just feet over the grass. "YOU CAN'T *DO* THAT!" the man screamed at the P-47s as they rumbled into the distance.

Lieutenant Wendell Pruitt and others had just completed the 332nd Fighter Group's first mission in the Jug, intercepting Bf-109s as they were attacking B-24 Liberator bombers near Udine on June 9, 1944. The young flyer had just downed one enemy aircraft; his companions had bagged four others.

On June 25, the Tuskegee flyers spotted a strange vessel in Trieste Harbor and dove through a thick blanket of flak to attack a German destroyer with everything they had. Unfortunately, "everything" was only their eight .50-caliber guns—they carried no rockets or bombs. Their fire was so withering, so accurate, that when they returned home, the pilots insisted they had

On the edge of a steel-mat runway, a pilot of the 325th Fighter Group awaits the order to fire up his engine. It took thirteen steps—levers, switches, and settings—to start a P-47's Double Wasp. Quickly, a combat pilot committed the list (and a hundred others) to memory. *The Museum of Flight, Champlin collection*

A few P-47s of the 325th Fighter Group were bare metal, like *Topper*, flown by Lt. Warren Penny. The markings were generally the same, with black aircraft numbers instead of the white seen on the olive drab-painted aircraft. *Stan Piet*

sunk the ship with their guns.

The brass was understandably skeptical. But there on Lt. Gwynne Pierson's gun camera film was the proof: hundreds of bright hits on the deck and superstructure of the ship and then a massive explosion that came nearly high enough to consume camera, aircraft, *and* pilot. It is a feat no other P-47 group can claim.

Only about a month after they acquired their Thun-

derbolts, the Tuskegee Airmen converted once again, this time receiving hand-me-down North American P-51 B- and C-models from another group. By mid-July 1944, the bleached, oft-patched, and exhaust-stained red-tailed razorback P-47 Thunderbolts that had served both the 325th and 332nd Fighter Groups so well were finally, mercifully, removed from the front lines.

FIGHTER-BOMBERS

Meanwhile, other American fighter groups assigned to the Mediterranean were also trading in their P-39s and P-40s for the venerable Republic fighter plane nicknamed, among other things, "Bucket of Bolts." And unlike the lucky pilots of the Checkertail Clan, the outfits coming online were more often than not involved in the fighter-bomber business rather than hunting for enemy airplanes.

The 57th Fighter Group was the first of these units, switched in early 1944 to the Thunderbolt to "move mud" as the pilots called it. In actuality, mud was well down on the target list. At the front lines, fighter-bomber units sought out enemy tanks, trucks, and troops. Farther beyond, they looked for airfields, tunnels, bridges, ammo dumps, and trains. When not working on their own, Thunderbolt units were involved in cleanups. After medium bombers worked over an airfield or rail yard, the Jugs would appear soon after, blast-

A little dog, picked up somewhere along the road in Italy, became a member of a P-47 group. Pilots were always good for a laugh: they named their feisty canine friend Focke-Wulf. The cowling looks to be that of a 57th Fighter Group Thunderbolt. *National Archives*

As seen from the troopers on the ground, a Thunderbolt of the 86th Fighter Group comes "down the chute" to deliver a pair of 500-pound bombs to enemy fortifications holding up the Allied advance. This action took place near Bologna in late 1944. *National Archives*

Plano Kid was a P-47D-30-RA Thunderbolt built in Evansville, Indiana. The plane was photographed in Italy. *The Museum of Flight, Taylor collection*

		Empty Weight:	10,000 pounds	
		Gross Weight:	14,500 pounds	
Model:	P-47D-30-RA	**Maximum Weight:**	17,500 pounds	
Number Built:	1,800			
Engine:	Pratt & Whitney	**Maximum Speed:**	423 mph at 30,000 feet	
	R-2800-59	**Landing Speed:**	105 mph	
Power Rating:	2,000/2,430 hp	**Service Ceiling:**	42,000 feet	
Propeller:	Curtiss Electric,	**Internal Fuel:**	370 gallons	
	13 feet diameter	**Maximum Range:**	1,030 miles at 10,000 feet	
Span:	40 feet 9.56 inches	**Armament:**	8 x .50-caliber	
Length:	36 feet 1.75 inches		machine guns,	
Height:	14 feet 8.13 inches		267 to 425 rounds per gun	
Wing Area:	300 square feet		2,500 pounds of bombs	

ing anything that the Allied bombs missed and causing havoc for enemy firefighting and rescue efforts.

The Thunderbolt drivers did the job with machine guns and various types of bombs, adding rocket tubes to their arsenal later in the year. Sporting three tubes on each wing, the rockets were said to possess the punch of a 105mm howitzer round. Early on, pilots were unimpressed with the rockets, which they judged as not very dependable or particularly accurate, if they *did* fire. However, the Allied infantrymen were amazed by the sight of the flame-spewing Jugs, and they related that when the HVARs flew true to their target, they did terrific damage against fortifications, trucks, and troops.

Another weapon was napalm bombs, external tanks filled with jellied gasoline with a grenade and fuse to set the mixture afire on impact. Dropped from above, the bombs created flaming blobs on the ground. When released at high speed and minimum altitude, the bombs made a fiery swath. They could be dropped near friendly troops with much less risk than regular high explosives and were deadly against enemy troops.

One final weapon employed against Axis soldiers was the 20-pound fragmentation anti-personnel bombs designed to spray thousands of bits of metal in every direction. The little bombs were grouped in a bundle with a metal shipping band. Pat Church, a 79th Fighter

Group pilot, was taxiing out for an attack while carrying these rigs on his Thunderbolt's wing pylons when a band broke, spilling the little bombs onto the runway. Church must have thought it was his lucky day: none of the bombs exploded. The ground crews quickly loaded another bundle to his wing, and back to the runway he went. The squadron ground crewmen had worked so fast and were so efficient that he could still make the mission.

As Church was gaining speed for takeoff, the second homemade bomb cluster snapped apart. This time a few of the spilling bombs detonated. Church's Jug, mortally wounded and burning, slid to a stop. Luckily, the P-47's wing absorbed much of the blast. The young flyer escaped with only slight burns. After crash crews snuffed out the fire, Church stepped forward to examine his fallen mount. The Thunderbolt would never fly again. He decided to remove the plane's clock from the instrument panel as a souvenir. When he looked in the cockpit, he found, once again, that the ground crews were fast and efficient. The clock had already vanished!

After dealing with liquid-cooled aircraft, most ground crews were pleased with the Thunderbolt and its relatively simple air-cooled Double Wasp. But the arrival of the Jug didn't mean an end to their long days; the P-47 brought new targets into range, and it could carry much, much more.

One pilot speculated that time once spent monkeying around with Warhawk and Airacobra Allison engines now went into feeding the Thunderbolt's insatiable appetite for weaponry. And when the Germans were pried from their holes and forced farther north, the brass couldn't pass up the chance to send Jug units into the fray three or four times a day.

Occasionally, escort missions took them northward, beyond Italy's "boot," and into southern France, Austria, and the Balkan states. There, they sometimes got the rare chance to do what every fighter pilot dreamt about: duel in the skies with Messerschmitts and Focke-Wulfs. But with the exception of the 325th Fighter Group, the P-47 units in the MTO did not produce a single ace pilot.

Somewhere in Italy, ground crewmen work elbow-deep in P-47 engine changes. Men who had been around a while said that the air-cooled Pratt & Whitneys were much easier to deal with than the liquid-cooled Allisons used in P-39 and P-40 fighters. *National Archives*

Headed north with a full complement of fuel, these Thunderbolts of the 350th Fighter Group were assigned to escort bombers flying to a bridge in Italy, just 10 miles from the Austrian border. *Torrid Tessie* was lost due to flak damage in April 1945. *National Archives*

They did, however, play an important role in the defeat of Italy and helped harass the German army as it slowly gave up ground.

During the Po Valley Campaign, the 350th Fighter Group history relates that "Fourteen hours a day the Thunderbolts are over the lines bombing, strafing, slamming rockets into German strong points, spreading flame over German bivouac areas, searching out individual guns or oxcarts or motorcyclists and pounding them relentlessly."

It might seem that the notion that an aviator in a seven-ton flying machine would bother with a solitary motorcycle is an exaggeration. But Thunderbolt pilots seemed to be attracted to the challenge. A motorbike was tiny, elusive, and fast. It took much more skill to get the rider than it did to blast a train or truck. One Jug pilot described discovering a pair of German soldiers driving a sidecar-equipped motorcycle. The pilot above and rider far below saw each other at approximately the same time, and the race was on. The rider was trying to hustle into a town up ahead, where there would be cover. But if you can't outrun a plummeting Thunderbolt in the air, you sure can't do it on the ground! The motorcyclist and

his companion knew they were losing the race and just as the P-47 began to fire, the motorcycle driver bailed out, leaving his passenger cowering in the sidecar. "So much for the Master Race!" the P-47 pilot later wrote.

More often, cutting vulnerable transportation lines was the job of the Thunderbolt groups. Bridges were natural bottlenecks that were high on the pilots' lists. Carrying 500- or 1,000-pound bombs, P-47 pilots found that sometimes a near miss did more damage than a direct hit on the bridge deck. Explosions in the water severely damaged the bridge's foundation and support structure, requiring huge amounts of work, if it could be fixed at all.

Using the gun sight to aim, a Thunderbolt pilot would roll into a steep dive, beginning his pullout at 1,500 feet. As the aim point disappeared under the long nose of the fighter, the pilot would toggle his bombs—commonly at one thousand feet. During the end of the run, many flyers chose to fire their guns to keep the enemy on the ground thinking about something other than shooting back. During a pullout, a pilot would often twist the plane almost inverted to observe the result of his attack, watching the bombs strike out of the rear of his canopy as he zoom-climbed into the sky.

Later, Thunderbolt pilots would fly bombs, rigged with delayed fuses, practically into a bridge at low level, pulling up at the last possible second. After the eight- to eleven-second delay, the bomb buried in the concrete would explode, perhaps bringing down the span.

Tunnels provided another target ripe to sever by accurate delivery of a few well-placed bombs. They were commonly very tricky to hit. By definition, most tunnels appeared in rough terrain and had dangerous obstacles directly over the aim point. High-flung rocks from explosions and even ricocheting delayed-fuse bombs

Col. Earl E. "Early" Bates Jr., 86th Fighter Group commander, near the distinctive red and white candy-striped tail of his Jug as he gets ready to fly a mission from Italy to targets in Southern France. *National Archives*

could come up and smash the attacker. Pilots compensated with curving approaches or more altitude. Luckily, as with bridges, a near miss could do the job as well as a hit. A cave-in or collapse often disrupted the flow of men and materials for long periods of time.

Later, some Thunderbolt flyers tried a different tunnel-busting technique. At fifty feet or less, flying at high speed, bomb-laden Jugs would approach the tunnel opening down the road or rail line. Pulling up and to the left, the P-47 pilot would toss his bombs toward the tunnel mouth. The second man would follow, conducting the same process once the smoke and debris cleared.

Some 79th Fighter Group Thunderbolt flyers went one further. One aircraft dropped a pair of 1,000-pound bombs into a tunnel's entrance, while another P-47 dropped two more on top. Together, the nearly simultaneous blasts of tons of high explosives were an Italian road worker's worst nightmare.

Sometimes, simply cutting often-traveled roads and rail lines created havoc. A skillfully placed 1,000-pounder made a crater in the middle of a main thoroughfare that displaced about forty truckloads of dirt. This kept enemy vehicles and men occupied with repair for the day instead of war-making.

The Thunderbolts actively searched for the trucks, too. The enemy had adjusted to the constant attack from above, so the pilots learned that the best time to find and flame convoys was dawn or dusk. The men who drove vehicles usually worked at night. But they could be found mounting up at sunset or caught a few miles from shelter as the sun came over the horizon in the morning.

Likewise, the Germans hid locomotives when not in use. However, there were only so many places for the enemy to conceal a big steam engine. Jugheads learned to follow side tracks, peeking in buildings, back alleys, and tunnels. Then it was time to let the lead fly. The bombing and strafing was risky, bringing aircraft down into the teeth of enemy defenses. Many planes were lost, and scores more damaged by enemy fire. The Thunderbolts flew so low that they often were struck by their own bomb fragments and parts of the equipment they decimated.

One pilot who briefly commanded the 79th Fighter Group suggested that he and his pilots could be more accurate dive-bombers if they waited to pull off the target at five hundred feet instead of one thousand. The others figured he must be nuts. Dirt, rocks, fire, and junk were all over the sky at one thousand feet when they attacked; any lower was just suicide.

On a road near Verona, two Thunderbolts pounce on traffic caught out in the open. As the first flyer pulls off in a climbing left turn, the trailing flyer captures the enemy trucks and his flight leader's P-47 (along with its shadow) in his gun camera during his strafing run. *National Archives*

Fearing for their lives, many 79th flyers were none too grief-stricken when their new commander was hit by flak and had to ditch in the water near Anzio. He was later captured. Some preferred to believe their leader was not hit by flak, but that the fatal damage was done by his own bomb, released too low over the target.

BATTLE DAMAGE

The enemy reluctantly gave up ground. The 350th Fighter Group, in particular, documented their fierce battles with enemy ground forces and antiaircraft emplacements with a series of astonishing photographs of mutilated P-47s that made it home when less robust fighters would have died on the spot. The unit history states, "The Hun faced the flights of the 350th with over 4,000 gun positions strategically placed throughout the battle area, and not counting his hundreds of mobile weapons. At least three quarters of our flights were fired upon, intensely."

While hunting German vehicles near Bologna, one Thunderbolt absorbed the impact of an 88mm shell in the wing. The projectile tore away the plane's airspeed indicator and left a huge hole but did not explode. Using all his strength, the pilot was able to recover and fly back to base.

Another Jug pilot did one better: he was hit by an 88mm gun while strafing—actually collided with the gun. The barrel of the German cannon left a huge gash in the Thunderbolt's tail. Back at the airfield, the crew chief had to artfully fill out his reports to hide the vital part of the story: "The damage was caused by an 88mm flak gun." He revealed no other details to those in authority.

Bombing and strafing an enemy command post, Lt. Samuel Allen Jr.'s P-47 was hit by a burst of antiaircraft

The 88mm antiaircraft shell shot in the direction of a 350th Fighter Group Thunderbolt hit its target, but plowed through the wing without exploding. Here, the pilot ponders his good fortune in the hole made by the massive projectile. *National Archives*

fire that completely tore away his right horizontal stabilizer and elevator. After he landed safely, he told his comrades that he was much less worried *this* time than on a previous mission where he had taken 40mm hits in the nose of his Jug that tore away two cylinders. That time, too, he had wrestled his big fighter all the way home and walked away unscathed.

While strafing gun positions, the P-47 of Lt. Edwin King took a flak blast, severing the main oil line to the engine. Gallons of the boiling black liquid soon covered his aircraft. Amazingly, even starved of oil, the Thunderbolt brought King back to base. With the aircraft literally covered in oil, he landed by flying in formation with a fellow pilot who acted as his forward vision. He was dirty at the end of the day, but unharmed. In photos, King stands frowning on his wing. His crew chief, the

Pilots agreed that the oil a P-47 carried worked best if it was contained on the *inside* of the plane. But Lt. Edwin King's Thunderbolt bucked the trend, continuing to operate with most of its vital fluid splashed all over the fuselage. The ground crews of the 350th Fighter Group had quite a job ahead of them to get this plane back into fighting shape. *National Archives*

As other Jugheads so eloquently put it, "Lieutenant Samuel Allen Jr. came back from a mission with his ass shot off." The 350th Fighter Group pilot returned home with no right side elevator or stabilizer. *The Museum of Flight*

airmen joked, was probably in a worse mood than King when he saw his filthy plane!

From September 1944 to the end of the war in Europe, aircraft of the 350th Fighter Group were hit 522 times by antiaircraft fire. Damaged planes returned to base 469 times.

Lieutenant Richard Sulzbach nearly did himself in, but his stout Thunderbolt failed to buy into his suicide attempt. He was strafing German trucks, and missing. Frustrated, he decided to take his Jug down low for a "can't miss" pass just a few feet above the ground. He mushed—an uncontrolled flight due to a partial stall—through a stand of trees. His P-47, appropriately named *Buzzin' Cousin*, emerged from the mess spitting branches. Once he landed, the men found Sulzbach glumly examining the crushed nose of his plane. The unit historian related, "The small, cocky pilot did not have his

usual grin on his face, and all he could say was, 'If I would have realized that boat was in that bad shape, I do not believe I would have brought her home.'"

Those who failed to come home often bailed out or crash-landed. A new pilot, Lt. Harold Wuest, of the 79th Fighter Group, had talked with veteran pilots about what he should do in emergency situations when he judged he couldn't make it home. One old hand explained the proper procedure for crash landing in the water: "After you hit the water, you stand up, walk out on the wing, inflate your raft, get in, and the plane will eventually sink."

Wuest was hit by ground fire on his third mission and forced to ditch in Venice Harbor. Just moments after the big Thunderbolt sloshed to a stop, it plunged under the waves, leaving him treading water. Wuest managed, with much difficulty, to climb into his raft. He was rescued three hours later.

Arriving back at base, Wuest sought out the veteran who claimed the P-47 would float. "Yeah, the same thing happened to me," the old pilot said to him casually. "But if I had told you the truth, you never would have ditched."

New pilots had to learn their trade in the P-47 "on the fly." As in other theaters, fresh pilots were expected to complete an amazingly accelerated schedule. Some flyers came from the U.S. with all their fighter-flying time in outdated P-40s. On the muddy fields of Italy, they were

Pilots said that Lt. Richard Sulzbach (left) was always smiling. The smile must have gone away for a while after his Thunderbolt plowed into the trees near Pisa, but being back on the ground, and safe, has made his grin come back. *National Archives*

given a Thunderbolt pilot's manual and left to sit in a P-47 cockpit to study. After a familiarization hop or two and perhaps four hours total time in the Jug, they were "appalled" to find themselves flying combat missions.

FOREIGN P-47 UNITS IN THE MTO

Some unique foreign units flew the P-47 in these battles alongside the Americans. French flyers who had fought with Hawker Hurricanes during the battles in North Africa were equipped with P-47Ds. The first unit, the *4ème Escadre de Chasse,* based on Corsica, consisted of approximately thirty-two aircraft. The number of French squadrons flying the P-47 continued to grow throughout 1944 and 1945 as they moved steadily northward with the fighting into France and Germany.

Another squadron established in the MTO was the *1 Grupo de Aviação de Caça,* whose pilots described the Thunderbolt as "avião pra macho" (a very masculine air-craft). These Brazilian Thunderbolt flyers were attached as a fourth squadron to the American 350th Fighter Group in October 1944. At the time, the 350th had itself just switched to the P-47 from the now-ancient Bell P-39.

The pilots of the 350th later said they admired the Brazilians and their eagerness to fight. One unit historian wrote that their "courage and tirelessness was dauntless." Some of the old hands who had been attacking ground targets for a while noted that their Brazilian friends pressed their attacks in a bit closer than they ever were willing to do.

Their planes mostly were painted in USAAF olive

Sergeant Govlart Ferreire makes a show of polishing the national insignia on the fuselage of one of Brazil's big green monsters. After the war, the surviving Thunderbolts the Brazilians had flown in combat made up their primary fighter force back home. *National Archives*

drab over gray, with the Brazilian national insignia and yellow and green rudder. A letter-and-number combination on the cowling denoted flight and aircraft designation.

The planes also bore an emblem unique to the Brazilians: an ostrich with a shield and gun, astride a cloud. The mascot was chosen after a comment made by one of the Brazilian pilots during his first time in the 350th's chow line in Italy. "Only an ostrich could live on this food," Capt. Fortunato de Oliveira supposedly exclaimed. Below the character were the words, "Senta a Pua!"—roughly translated "Let 'em have it!"

And they did, throwing over one million rounds of .50-caliber ammunition, 4,400 bombs, and 850 rockets at the enemy during more than 2,500 offensive sorties. After the war, twenty-six of their combat-used Thunderbolts were shipped to South America to make up the cornerstone of the *Força Aérea Brasileira*.

RAYMOND KNIGHT

One Brazilian aircraft that didn't make it home was a Thunderbolt borrowed by Lt. Raymond Knight of the 350th Fighter Group. Late in the war, British and American armies had broken through in the Apennines in Northern Italy. As the Germans retreated across the Po River Valley to the Alps, P-47 units were sent into the fray, often three or four times a day. Knight and other members of the 350th had been working for days— attacking, refueling, rearming, and then back to the shooting gallery of the valley.

But the gunfire went both ways. Knight's aggressive style and attacks right down on the deck had cost him his aircraft. His P-47 was shot up badly, but Knight knew it was valuable to his unit during this critical point in the battle for Italy. He nursed the dying plane back to Pisa. Once he'd landed, Knight's crew chief gave him the bad news: his plane was so ravaged it would be weeks before it flew again, if it *ever* flew again.

He and his superiors negotiated a deal with the Brazilians, who pulled a fairly new Thunderbolt from the line and awarded it to Knight for the next day's flight. The men of his squadron stayed up that night, changing the plane's insignia, aircraft numbers, and markings to those of a 350th Fighter Group, 346th Fighter Squadron. They even painted Knight's nose art, *Oh Johnnie*, below the cockpit.

As day dawned, Knight, who had shown exceptional skill in beating up enemy airfields, volunteered to lead a group of Thunderbolts to a German airbase at Ghedi. Destroying German aircraft was essential if the Allied armies were to continue their advance. At the target, Knight left the others above and dove down at high speed through murderous antiaircraft fire to scout out the locations of aircraft hidden around the field's perimeter. Once they'd coordinated their attack, Knight

In his mud-caked boots, Master Sgt. Robson Saldanaha poses on the wing of a Thunderbolt operated by the Brazilians in Italy. The art on the side of the aircraft was inspired by the lousy cooking they were served while living overseas with the Americans. *National Archives*

and the others came down, guns blazing. Knight destroyed five German bombers on his own; his flight accounted for two more.

After his return to Pisa, Knight, with three others, headed toward the airfield at Bergamo, known for intense and accurate antiaircraft fire. While his men cruised above, Knight discovered a gaggle of fighters and bombers under camouflaged netting surrounding the field. In an area where two strafing passes were suicide, Raymond Knight conducted ten. His hearty Thunderbolt caught repeated barrages of gunfire but continued to fly. His own efforts left six bombers and two fighters burning, while his comrades added more.

During a "smoke and a Coke" between missions on this day of heavy fighting, someone told Charles Gilbert, Knight's squadron leader, about the young lieutenant's all-out war against the German air force. Gilbert asked the intelligence officer to write up Knight for the Distin-

When he heard what had happened, Charles Gilbert amended the DSC recommendation to the Medal of Honor. Knight was one of only two P-47 pilots to receive the nation's highest award for valor. Years later Gilbert wrote, "Ray Knight was an exceptional man, an unassuming taciturn Texan. His fighting career was nothing short of spectacular. Ray is buried in the military cemetery outside Pisa. I hope any Jug pilots passing through the vicinity will pay appropriate tribute to a great guy."

Lieutenant Raymond Knight (right) of the 350th Fighter Group stands next to his crew chief and their flak-spattered Thunderbolt. He was exceptionally skilled at attacking enemy airfields, and he often gathered non-lethal damage to his aircraft in the process. In April 1945 his luck ran out. *National Museum of the United States Air Force*

Careful study of these 350th Fighter Group Jugs flying over the Apennines gives one a good idea of the attrition rate among fighter-bomber units. The plane nearest to the camera and the flight leader's aircraft are veterans. The middle two are new; one has the start of squadron markings, and the other is yet to have anything at all. The machine in the foreground was written off after a belly landing a month after this photo was taken. *National Archives*

guished Service Cross (DSC). Meanwhile, crews worked into the night repairing the flak-spattered *Oh Johnnie* for another day of battle.

As dawn broke on April 25, 1945, the silence at Bergamo was broken by the roar of *Oh Johnnie*'s engine, followed close behind by three other P-47s. The Americans buzz-sawed an additional trio of parked German bombers, but the price was high: Knight's plane was hit in the left wing root by a German 88mm round.

Pulling off the target, the Jug was still flying, but Ray Knight could barely control the fighter, and he could only get 160 miles per hour out of the wounded ship. Knight's men tried to convince him to bail out over friendly territory, but in the end, he refused. His unit needed his plane to come home. He tried to make it through a low point in the Apennines to Pisa.

Knight and his wingman started through the 5,000-foot pass at 5,200 feet. At the south end of the pass, just twenty-five miles from home, Knight's damaged plane was caught in the mountain winds, and he lost control. He tried to jump, but it was too late.

In France, Ninth Air Force pilots catch a quick bite to eat, using the tail of a worn Thunderbolt as their lunch table. The pilot on the right wears a silk scarf. This piece of flight gear was not only a traditional part of a flyer's garb, it helped protect the neck from chafing as the pilot constantly scanned the skies, looking for enemy aircraft. *National Archives*

Captain Raymond Walsh flies through a storm of flames and debris as the vehicle he was strafing explodes in a huge fireball. The German truck convoy was carrying ammunition, creating the huge blast. Luckily, Walsh's Thunderbolt stayed in one piece, bringing him safely home. *National Archives*

CHAPTER SIX
GROUND POUNDERS: P-47 FIGHTER-BOMBERS IN EUROPE

Based in the Middle East and then England, the Ninth Air Force would earn fame in the latter part of World War II chasing the German army ever homeward on the Continent. A large part of the punching power of this tactical air force came from Thunderbolt fighters and their pilots, trained to wreak havoc among retreating Nazi armor and soldiers.

OVER THE CHANNEL

Flyers of the Ninth Air Force discovered early that the England-based pilots had it pretty good. The Thunderbolt airmen of the Eighth occasionally were on hand when the Luftwaffe whipped itself into a frenzy and took a serious shot at them. Famous ace fighter pilots like Hubert "Hub" Zemke or Francis "Gabby" Gabreski were Eighth Air Force men—guys you might see on the cover of *Life* magazine.

Who had ever heard of Edwin Fisher, Robert Coffey, or John Wainright? That's what it was like in the Ninth Air Force. The Germans shot at them just the same, but there were no worries the American public was going to miss these flyers if they cashed in their chips. And the

chance to show their prowess in air-to-air combat was rare, if it came at all.

And what about after the flyer coaxed his battered Jug home after a long day? On the English side of the Channel, there was a nice airfield, a real roof to sleep under, and maybe even a pub. Heck, Eighth Air Force pilots even mingled with *girls* in the evenings. Not so in the tiny airfields hacked into French soil on the fighting side of the water. It could be awfully gloomy and cold in a canvas tent near enough to the front lines that flyers sometimes could hear small-arms fire in the distance. As one Thunderbolt pilot wrote, "It's always the little things. Flak, enemy fighters, we could handle. But soggy ice cream, wet socks, and no letter from home were hard to take."

The first Allied airfield in France was started just hours after the June 6, 1944 invasion, near Utah Beach. By the 19th, there were fighters based on the French side of the pond. By August, the bulk of the Ninth Air Force's fighter units were operating from short, steel-matted strips which commonly had codes instead of names—such as A-3 (Cardonville) or A-10 (Carentan).

Takeoff loaded with bombs and extra fuel was usually

Flyers of the Eighth Air Force, like Francis Gabreski, got all the publicity while Ninth Air Force Thunderbolt pilots lugged bombs to the front lines, hardly ever encountering the Luftwaffe. While the Eighth Air Force fighter pilots defended the bombers in the air, the Ninth worked closely with Allied ground forces to push enemy armies back into Germany. *National Archives*

a stressful experience on the short, hastily improvised fighter strips, especially after it had rained. A flyer named Jack Reynolds of the 373rd Fighter Group recalls a spoof, "Rules for Takeoff," posted in the ops office:

1. Line up on the runway with the canopy open.
2. Stand on the brakes.
3. Pull the stick all the way back.
4. Push the throttle, mixture, prop control, and turbo to the firewall.
5. When the tail comes off the ground, ease off the brakes and push the stick forward so you are moving with the tail in the air.
6. With one hand on the throttle quadrant.
7. With one hand on the bomb release.
8. With one hand on the wheel retract handle.
9. With one hand on the cowl-flap closer handle.
10. With one hand on the elevator trim wheel.
11. With one hand on the safety belt release.
12. With one hand on the water-injection button.
13. And with one hand, cross yourself.
14. When you reach the end of the runway, ease the stick back and retract the wheels.

Some "locals" come out to survey flight operations of the 50th Fighter Group at A-10 near Carentan after the Allies have come asho France. *National Archives*

Army engineers try to sweep the slime off a wire-mesh landing field. Operating from primitive fighter strips in France, ground crews often had to move mud after the rains. *National Archives*

The first fight, before ever leaving the ground, was with the constant mud or dust. As crew chiefs sat on the wing directing taxiing Thunderbolts, the heavy planes squeezed mud and water up through the pierced steel planking. In the summer, it was an annoyance. Pilots tapped their brakes after takeoff, and the muddy wheels stopped spinning and closed up into the wells without too much trouble. As it grew colder, Jug flyers learned to come down to low altitude for "thaw time" at the end of the mission, to melt the slushy mass of dirt and ice in their wings before lowering the gear.

In flight, pilots found that even the most careful crew chief usually tracked dirt and clods of mud into the cockpit while the plane was being attended to on the ground. After coming off a bombing run and rolling nearly upside down, many a Thunderbolt pilot was showered with filth. They were ordered to wear goggles at all times. Occasionally, Thunderbolt flyers would open their canopies and do a few preemptive barrel rolls to clear the floor.

Once in the air, usually armed with bombs, the Ninth Air Force men took on many of the same types of missions as Thunderbolt fighter-bomber pilots in Italy. Supporting Allied troops, they would strafe and blast away enemy strong points. Beyond the lines, nearly anything used by the German army was fair game: fixed targets like bridges and airfields as well as vehicles, armor, and supply barges.

Before D-Day, many fighter-bomber missions targeted the French transportation system, to lessen the German response once Allied soldiers came ashore. In the weeks after the invasion, P-47 flyers concentrated on hitting German tanks, which posed a serious threat to Allied troops should they be allowed to make it to the

Captain Kent Geyer carefully paints a bridge on the side of his P-47 after his bombs sent one crashing into the river below. Above the bridge are the results of his other missions: severed railroad lines and a pair of German fighters. *National Archives*

The American Third Army came across these two German tanks, victims of air attacks, as they advanced though Belgium. The tank in the foreground has a thrown track. The other machine, a Panther, was the heavier of the two and much more difficult to stop. *National Archives*

front lines. It was a challenge to drop bombs close enough to disable a powerful armored machine.

The Thunderbolt's armor-piercing rounds inflicted tremendous damage. Flyers had seen holes left by API rounds that had been propelled through the steel rails of train tracks. But even a solid burst of .50-caliber would not often penetrate a Panther or Tiger's thick armor. Fighter-bomber pilots found there were other ways to kill a tank. Blasting the tracks or drive wheels could disable the behemoths. Or a concentrated shot into the rear deck of the vehicle could sometimes propel slugs down through the ventilation louvers and into the engine. Another angle, so to speak, was to bounce bursts off the ground into the monster's belly when tanks were traveling on a hard surface. Here the armor was the thinnest, and once the rounds penetrated the floor, the heavy armor contained them instead of letting them out. As one Jug pilot wrote, "It tears the hell out of everything and everybody in there as it flies around like a buzz saw."

Allied air attacks exploited another vulnerability: they blasted to oblivion trains and trucks transporting gasoline whenever they found them. Many Panzer units were forced to carry their own fuel supply to the front by

Soldiers pushing forward near the front found this German staff car, absolutely devastated by strafing Jabos. Motorcycles and single autos were not small enough to escape the constant attack by the Ninth Air Force's sky predators. *National Archives*

The thirty-second Republic employees' war bond plane, *Frenchie*, a P-47D-22-RE, in Iceland on September 27, 1944. *National Archives*

Model:	P-47D-22-RE	Empty Weight:	9,900 pounds
Number Built:	850	Gross Weight:	13,500 pounds
Engine:	Pratt & Whitney R-2800-59	Maximum Weight:	15,000 pounds
Power Rating:	2,000/2,300 hp		
Propeller:	Hamilton Standard Hydro-matic, 13 feet 1.88 inches diameter	Maximum Speed:	435 mph at 30,000 feet
		Landing Speed:	104 mph
		Service Ceiling:	42,000 feet
		Internal Fuel:	305 gallons
Span:	40 feet 9.56 inches	Maximum Range:	835 miles at 10,000 feet
Length:	35 feet 10 inches		
Height:	14 feet 9.13 inches	Armament:	8 x .50-caliber machine guns,
Wing Area:	300 square feet		267 to 425 rounds per gun
			2 x 1,000-pound bombs or
			3 x 500-pound bombs

towing a trailer or strapping jerry cans outside of the vehicle's hull. Ruptured fuel tanks mixed with sparks from striking rounds or the tank's own hot exhaust could result in a catastrophic fire. While the other methods often left the Jug driver wondering if the tank's crew was simply playing dead, a big fire was a sure thing. Hatches popped open, crewmen scattered, and the vehicle ignited like a box of firecrackers.

Striking truck convoys was equally rewarding. A Thunderbolt's guns could rip apart the light-skinned vehicles with ease. P-47 pilots learned to approach columns (as well as trains) from the side instead of head-on. Attacking from either end of the row forced each Thunderbolt to dive one at a time along a predictable pathway. This enabled the enemy to accurately

direct their gunfire. Approaching from the side, P-47s could bore in from anywhere, often in pairs or more. This tactic forced the defenders to divide their firepower.

Jug pilots' love of hunting staff cars and motorcycle dispatch riders continued into France as well. One flyer called it "great sport." Once, four flights of Thunderbolts were hefting 500-pound bombs and looking for something worthwhile in their assigned sector to hit. Nothing—and fuel was running low. Finally, a single German motorcyclist came into view on the road below, and the flight leader said, "Oh, what the hell."

One after the other, sixteen Jugs went down the chute, tossing bombs at the speeding rider, who could do nothing but twist his throttle grip all the way back and keep going. He survived the thirty-two bombs lobbed his way, and countless bursts of machine gun fire. And, when he got to his destination, he had one heck of a story to tell his comrades!

On another occasion, a P-47 pilot was departing an area where he'd been shooting up a convoy of trucks. Right in front of him, on the road, was a motorcyclist. But the Thunderbolt flyer had used nearly all his ammunition on the trucks down the road. When he pressed the button on the top of the control stick, only a single tracer bullet leapt from his guns—he had no more ammunition. The lone tracer crashed into the road near the motorcycle's front tire. The sudden puff of dust spooked the German rider, who crashed into a wall. It was an accident that the motorcyclist did not survive, said the flyer.

GRIM BUSINESS

Hunting men and machines on the ground was a grim business. Instead of looking at one's victim as just another aircraft (albeit with a pilot), Thunderbolt fighter-bomber pilots could see the results of their actions up close. One flyer described how his flight disabled a train in a snow-covered field and watched as hundreds of German soldiers piled out of the boxcars and into the high drifts on the sides of the tracks. There was nowhere for them to go. The snow was too deep. There was no debate among the P-47 pilots. Not even a hesitation. They made flight school style gunnery passes one after the other, over and over, until every bullet they carried was gone.

The Thunderbolts were wreaking havoc over France. Germans who went out during the day were taking their lives in their hands. The P-47s seemed like vultures, watching and waiting for a chance to swoop. The Germans even had a name for the plane that made their lives miserable—*Jabo*, short for *Jagdbomber* (fighter-bomber). Rumours suggested that captured Jabo pilots, so hated for their deeds, were considered war criminals and shot, instead of being treated as prisoners of war.

The basic instructions to new P-47 flyers were, "If you have to bail out, try and do it over a Luftwaffe base. They'll treat you fair." And there was a caveat: "But try not to bail out over the airfield you and your buddies were just strafing. They may not see the humor in it." Indeed, the farther behind the lines a pilot came down, the less his fellow Thunderbolt pilots would help him get away. Lowering the boom on German soldiers tasked with retrieving a downed American pilot made them more than a little angry when the survivors finally reached their man.

When forced to bail out, Jug flyers often ditched their flying gear and lied about their particular vocation when questioned. A whole lot of "B-24 pilots" suddenly

For German ground troops, it must have felt like the devil was tracking their every move—and here's the proof. Louis Houck, a young squadron commander of the 365th Fighter Group, the Hell Hawks, in his RAF-type helmet complete with "field mod" devil horns. *National Archives*

appeared in German hands, not a *Jabo Flieger* in the bunch, after a particularly luckless attack on an enemy airfield.

One captured Thunderbolt pilot related a story to his fellow prisoners, the remains of a B-17 crew, as they were being transported to a prison camp. He told the men, "I almost got away." It had happened on a train platform in a fairly large city in Germany. He and the young Nazi guard assigned to him were waiting for the train. After a train came into the station, hundreds of civilians streamed from the cars.

The captured pilot decided to briskly step away into the crush of people. His guard, like him, was fairly short; it was going to be easy to lose him in this huge crowd. It was a mistake, and the P-47 pilot, still in his muddy American-made flight suit, knew it before he'd taken ten steps. Amid the cold stares from the German people in the jostling crowd, he felt there was a good chance he might not make it out to the street alive, let alone get home to his comrades.

He began to hop up into the air, looking for his German guard over the masses. Nothing. He started to rotate as he pogoed, looking in every direction. Nine o'clock—nothing. Six o'clock and three o'clock—nope. Then, at the apex of one of his jumps, he caught sight of the young Nazi guard, who was also hopping up and down. He strolled the fifteen feet that separated them. They were both overjoyed to be reunited.

DARK HUMOR

Many pilots were shot down and killed or captured in the hazardous skies above retreating Nazi forces. But, as in the past, the Thunderbolt brought back flyers who *should have* been dead. At the airfield, it was often considered more of a joke than a close call. Young fighter pilots, who considered themselves invincible, didn't grasp the gravity of the situation. Historian Stephen Ambrose once wrote, "It was generally felt that by the time he reached his mid-twenties, a man was too sensible to take the chances routinely required of a P-47 pilot."

They'd laugh about how three planes of Red Flight were speeding along just feet off the ground when the lead aircraft encountered high-tension wires. In a split second, Red One jerked back on his stick and went over. Red Two just squeaked under the humming wires with a few feet to spare. Red Three plowed right through them while trying to decide. It *was* slightly funny, in a morbid sort of way, when a P-47 came home dragging twenty-five feet of cable.

Back home in Belgium, Staff Sgt. Robert Rakow ruefully examines the damage done to a Thunderbolt named *I'll Get By*. Flown by 404th Fighter Group commander Lt. Col. Leo Moon, the plane was hit while attacking trains southeast of Coblenz, Germany. *National Archives*

In a similar tale, seemingly exaggerated to showcase the Jug's survivability, four Thunderbolts were coming home in murky weather and happened to fly over a French town at low level. The first plane hit the church steeple at the top, knocking off the finial. The second fighter chipped off the top two feet of the steeple, leaving a dent in the wing. The third plane hacked off another five feet. The fighter was battered and twisted but landed okay. Of course, the fourth P-47 hit the steeple head-on near its base. But it too came chugging in to land, covered in shingles and carrying huge pieces of lumber lodged in its wings.

Flipped during takeoff from a muddy Belgian field, this P-47's bombs are still in their shackles. The pilot had to be dug from the cockpit, but emerged only "slightly hurt." The guns have been emptied and the bomb's fuses removed before the wrecker comes in to recover the Thunderbolt carcass. *National Archives*

Jack Reynolds of the 373rd Fighter Group recalled the failed takeoff of Lt. Ted Buckley, who hit a crater during his run and flipped the Thunderbolt, leaving the cockpit buried in the ground. "We found him drenched with gasoline, hanging upside down in his harness and cursing like a fiend," related Reynolds. "Before we had time to do anything, Lt. Ramon Franzalia from group headquarters ran in under the wing, drew his .45 automatic, pointed it at Buckley's head, and shouted, 'Don't worry, Buck. If it starts to burn, I'll shoot you!'"

"The rest of us lifted the tail, opened the canopy, and released ole Buck. He got out, swore at Franzalia, and lunged toward him . . . but fell into the mud. Franzalia took off running and wasn't seen for two days . . . until Buck had cooled down."

ACROSS THE CONTINENT

There were some notable missions for Ninth Air Force pilots that went beyond strafing and bombing. In late June, Capt. Raymond Walsh of the 406th Fighter Group was startled to see a German V-1 "buzz bomb" cruise in front of his nose. He gave chase and pulled to within three hundred yards of the pulsejet-powered flying bomb. He fired at the unmanned missile and watched as it fell to one side and dove into the English Channel.

Interestingly, Walsh's Thunderbolt appeared in one of the most famous images of the fighter-bomber war in Europe. He and his wingman were attacking trucks when one exploded in a huge ball of flame. Walsh had hit the ammunition truck while his wingman, trailing behind, captured the image with his gun camera. In the scene, Walsh's Thunderbolt is about to plunge through a one-hundred-foot wall of fire and debris. Amazingly, Raymond Walsh and his plane returned to base safely.

Over Holland in September 1944, Lt. John Wain-

Bullets slam into the nose of this Messerschmitt caught by a Ninth Air Force Thunderbolt at fairly low level. Due to the rarity of encountering German aircraft, fighter-bomber pilots always aggressively pursued the planes they could scare up during a mission. *National Archives*

wright and his comrades in the 404th Fighter Group found themselves in a comparatively rare situation for Ninth Air Force pilots—in the middle of a dogfight with German aircraft. Turning into three Bf-109s, Wainwright fired at one as he passed, head on. It exploded. The blast of the enemy's prop wash sent the Thunderbolt into a spin. When he recovered at eighteen thousand feet, another Messerschmitt was flying right out in front of his nose. He fired, and the second Nazi fighter burst into flames.

Alone now, Wainwright spotted two more German fighters boring in on him. His violent turn to evade them sent him into another spin. Again, when he recovered, his opponents were laid out in front of his diving P-47. Later admitting he was too shook-up to take careful aim, he sprayed the sky with tracers.

The pair of German pilots must have seen Wainwright's bullets. In their haste to make a quick exit, the two collided, exploding in a shower of debris. Wainwright pulled back hard on the stick, momentarily blacking out. He recovered at six thousand feet.

Cruising for home, the flyer saw two more Bf-109s quickly closing on him. He banked left in a hard turn, heading for a cloud bank as they fired at him. He turned to take what he thought would be his last look and was startled to find a black plume where the fighters had been. Apparently, these two fighters had also collided as they jockeyed to get on Wainwright's tail.

He pointed his nose at the wreckage, capturing with his gun camera an image of three dismembered black-crossed wings flipping end over end in their plunge to the ground. John Wainwright received the Distinguished Service Cross for destroying six aircraft in the strange encounter.

HUNTING LOCOMOTIVES

Most fighter-bomber pilots of the Ninth Air Force would never know the thrill of air-to-air combat as they slowly leap-frogged from one muddy airfield to another in constant pursuit of enemy ground forces. They took their aggressions out on what they could find on the ground.

At a train crossing near Normandy, the bullets of an attacking P-47 of the 405th Fighter Group slam into the cab and boiler of a moving locomotive. In this one frame of film taken from Capt. Charles Mohrle's gun camera, at least eight API rounds, leaving bright blasts, can be seen striking the train. *Author's collection*

Among the more common targets were locomotives. At first, it was easy: blast the steam engine, the train coasted to a stop, and then it was a turkey shoot on the cars. The destruction of a locomotive was a spectacular sight a Thunderbolt pilot could see from the air, even at several hundred miles per hour. A plume of steam gushing skyward was the sign that the rout was about to begin. Bombs might be used to knock the train off the tracks or sever the line, making more problems for the Germans.

Then it happened. During a typical free-for-all came intense ground fire, seemingly from nowhere. Someone in the ranks of the Third Reich had come up with a brilliant idea, and "loco hunting" was never the same. The Germans began protecting the trains with Quad 20mm flak guns on flatcars, and, even more insidious, positioned them inside boxcar-looking rigs with collapsible sides. Pilots called them "flak wagons." Often, the flak gunners would wait to expose themselves. Once the engine was blown and anxious Thunderbolt pilots moved in close, the gunners would open up.

The Jug pilots countered with tactics of their own: more speed, more distance between aircraft, and an always-wary eye toward a seemingly helpless line of boxcars. Soon, flight leaders took out the engine, while wingmen dueled with the gunners simultaneously. "That worked okay," said Bill Colgan of the 79th Fighter Group. "If *anything* about a shootout with flak guns is ever okay!"

Some Thunderbolt drivers came up with another "clean and painless" way to rid themselves of trains if the conditions were right. Orbiting nearby, they'd wait for the engine and its line of cars to lumber into a tunnel. Then they tried to seal both ends with bombs.

Train crews, truck drivers, tankers, and soldiers on the Axis side of the lines all knew that when the Jabos appeared overhead, their nightmares were about to come true.

INTO GERMANY

Over time, the Allied ground forces, coupled with savage air attacks, pushed into Germany. Some German troops survived the fighting and retreated through what they glumly called the *Jabo Rennstrecke* (the fighter-bomber race course) of France. Many departed in trucks, driving in groups of three or four, at night, and at five-hundred-yard intervals—all to foil the ever-present Thunderbolts seen in the daylight hours.

There was debate among the Thunderbolt pilots about what constituted a valid target within the enemy's

This is the grave of a P-47 pilot who was caught in an ammunition explosion during a strafing pass and crashed in the German countryside. A refugee Frenchman and his wife created the site, *within* Germany, to honor the fallen American airman. *National Archives*

homeland. Were civilian activities they saw on the ground fair game? Was a cow or a farmer or a village worth shooting? And, was it morally acceptable? Most flyers said no.

But there were exceptions. After a group of Thunderbolt pilots heard reports that one of their own had been killed by German civilians, they turned on non-military areas in retaliation. Though civilians were never the primary target, if it was necessary to jettison bombs at the end of a mission, these flyers let them go over a German town or village instead of an open field. One pilot of the group wrote, "War brings out the absolute worst in the men who do the fighting."

The Germans had abandoned many of their airfields because of the attacks and were now sometimes flying aircraft from sections of the autobahn. Thunderbolt pilots flew low, often amid heavy ground fire, to ferret them out. One clue was a paved median strip between the lanes, often painted green or dirty brown to look as if it were unsuitable for flight operations. Some of the medians even had trees, presumably sunk into holes and removed when German aircraft used the makeshift fields.

Another tactic was to look for aircraft under camouflaged netting in the woods beside the roads. An observant

Jug flyer might spot the nose of a propeller-driven Focke-Wulf or Messerschmitt protruding from the trees. Thunderbolt pilots particularly prized jet-powered Messerschmitt Me-262 fighter planes.

However, the Germans distributed the aircraft as much as possible, sometimes many miles from their take-off locations. A simple flying accident sometimes blew the cover on a large, clandestine flight operation. A disabled German fighter on the side of the road attracted eager Jabo flyers in droves. Peering into the tall trees, they were often rewarded with a wealth of other, better hidden enemy airplanes.

The first American fighters of the Ninth Air Force to occupy a German airfield were the Thunderbolts of the 365th Fighter Group, which moved into airfield Y-46 in Aachen on March 16, 1945. The field was a sloppy mud pool near the Belgian/German border, and the American airmen cursed their beaten and battered foes for not maintaining it better.

Even though the war in Europe was clearly coming to an end, Thunderbolts still went up day after day, looking for targets. Amidst the dreary and risky ground-attack missions, a few flyers of the Ninth Air Force managed to add to their air-to-air tallies in April.

Lieutenant Edward Edwards of the 373rd Fighter Group was strafing Sachau airfield in Germany when he and his companions ran into a gaggle of airborne Fw-190s. Edwards shot down four that day, bringing his total for the war to five and a half.

A D-model Jug of the 358th Fighter Group cruises over Germany late in the war. Complementing its nose art, *That's Urass* has a row of kicking donkeys on the cowl flaps. *National Archives*

A 27th Fighter Group P-47 Thunderbolt, *Mary*, sits parked at a German airfield overrun by the Allies as the war in Europe came to a close. *The Museum of Flight, Champlin collection*

A Thunderbolt of the 368th Fighter Group flying high above the Bavarian Alps after the war ended. Lieutenant George McWilliams hadn't accrued enough points to go home, so he was stuck as part of the occupation force. *Stan Piet*

Elsewhere, Lt. Melvyn Paisley of the 366th Fighter Group got his last "half kill" of the war the hard way. Near Potsdam, he and his wingman dropped in on a Focke-Wulf from above. Gaining speed rapidly, as P-47s were known to do, Paisley passed in front of the German fighter. The hunter became the hunted.

The gung-ho Jug flyer's wingman, Paul Ollerton, managed to stay behind the enemy fighter and began blasting away as the Focke-Wulf, in turn, honed in on Paisley. Ollerton's bullets hosed down both planes—the Focke-

Wulf went down and Paisley's hearty Jug absorbed many .50-caliber slugs but kept flying. Ollerton, perhaps mortified by his near kill of his own flight mate, decided to share his victory with Paisley.

On May 8, 1945, the battles in Europe ended. Among the Thunderbolt pilots, new questions arose. Would they be sent home, stay in Germany, or would they be sent to the Pacific to finish off the Japanese?

It's going to take some work to remove this P-47D from its resting place. It appears that the plane ran out of runway, the pilot stomping on the brakes when it was too late. The unusual attitude gives a good view of the black stripes on the fuselage and wings, applied to Allied fighters operating in and around the Philippines. *The Museum of Flight, Bowers collection*

Neel Kearby leads a flight of eight 348th Fighter Group Thunderbolts over the Pacific early in the group's operational career. At a time when the top brass in the southwest Pacific didn't want the P-47, Kearby's men took on veteran Japanese flyers, scoring many victories. *The Museum of Flight, Champlin collection*

CHAPTER SEVEN

ISLAND HOPPERS: P-47s OVER THE PACIFIC

The Pacific war was different than the fighting in Europe and the Mediterranean, but the army's P-47 Thunderbolt was thrown into the fray just the same. Conditions were difficult for a heavy, land-based fighter, and many of the same problems the P-47 experienced in Europe were only amplified in the Pacific. Range and fuel consumption issues plagued Thunderbolt groups for much of the war, and in an environment in which miles and miles of empty sea separated islands, airfields, and hot spots, the fuel-thirsty fighter made pilots very nervous.

The Japanese front-line fighters worried them too. The prolific Mitsubishi A6M Zero fighter and Nakajima Ki-43, codenamed respectively Zeke and Oscar by Allied intelligence, were even smaller and more agile than Germany's Bf-109 and Fw-190. Even more than in Europe, the P-47 pilot learned to play to his plane's strengths.

As with other U.S.-built fighters like the Lockheed P-38 and Curtiss P-40, airmen used the Thunderbolt's advantages in speed, power, and firepower to defeat a more nimble foe. "Don't ever get into a turning dogfight with a Zero," flyers cautioned, "or there's a good chance you won't be coming home." They resorted to slash-and-run tactics: diving in on an enemy from above and climbing away at full power. Generally, Japanese planes were not well armored, and early versions had no self-sealing fuel tanks, allowing the P-47's eight .50-calibers to do tremendous damage. Then, assuming there was more fighting to be done, a Thunderbolt pilot would climb out of range before swooping down again. As German flyers had come to realize over Europe, when a Jug dropped onto your tail from a long dive, there was little chance for escape.

Altitude was another factor. The lower a Thunderbolt flew, said pilots, the more its truck-like qualities seemed to show. Around twenty thousand feet was the optimum altitude for fuel consumption, so that's where most P-47s traveled, rarely venturing higher than twenty-five thousand. At that altitude, there was less vertical room to set up the slashing attacks to defeat more lithe fighters. And the Thunderbolt's sure-fire escape route—roll over and dive—did a flyer little good if he was too close to the ocean surface to build up speed.

The Thunderbolt had good traits for fighting in the Pacific as well. The plane's rugged construction and toughness were great advantages when operating from primitive dirt and coral runways. Its air-cooled engine worked well even in hot, humid conditions. And, as it had elsewhere, the Thunderbolt was often pushed into the fighter-bomber role. Near the ground, in the teeth of the Japanese gunfire, these favorable characteristics helped bring many a P-47 pilot home alive.

NEW GUINEA

In the bleak first months of World War II in the South Pacific, the U.S. Army desperately needed fighters; preferably long-range, twin-engine P-38 Lightnings. The commander of the Fifth Air Force, Gen. George Kenney, could hardly acquire anything at all. The Allies had chosen to focus on the battles in Europe.

Offered a P-47 group, he took it, and many under his command were mortified. They said the P-47 Thunderbolt was unsuited for their theater of war. Range and size made it a poor match for both its environs and opponents. Fortunately for Kenney, the naysayers failed to faze the commander of the first P-47 outfit in the Pacific, the 348th Fighter Group. When the first Thunderbolts came to Port Moresby, New Guinea, in mid-1943, the group's commander, Lt. Col. Neel Kearby, immediately inquired about the whereabouts of Japanese aircraft, looking to get his men and planes into the fight.

Neel Kearby earned the Medal of Honor for dispatching six Japanese fighters during one mission in 1943. Sadly, the ace who had pioneered the use of the Thunderbolt in the Southwest Pacific was killed in combat on March 5, 1944. *The Museum of Flight, American Fighter Aces Association*

While waiting for suitable auxiliary fuel tanks from the United States, Kearby acquired handmade 200-gallon tanks from Australia. The extra fuel increased the Thunderbolt's range from 200 to 320 miles. While it was a remarkable technical feat, Kearby simply saw the new homemade tanks as his unit's ticket to going farther, staying longer, and *fighting more.*

A 348th Fighter Group aircraft carrying a bulbous 200-gallon drop tank produced in Australia. Without the range to aggressively pursue the Japanese, and with the arrival of American-made tanks months away, Kearby resorted to homemade affairs. *The Museum of Flight, Champlin collection*

And fight they did. During their first six months, there were many targets for the eager American flyers. Over New Guinea's jungle terrain, Kearby's Thunderbolts materialized above Japanese planes and airfields, seemingly always with a speed and altitude advantage. During the last months of 1943, the group shot down 150 enemy aircraft while losing only eight pilots.

One of the most successful engagements occurred October 11, as four 348th fighters dove on an airfield near Wewak. Kearby, leading the flight, shot down a Zeke and then discovered a huge group of airborne Oscar and Kawasaki Ki-61 Tony fighter planes escorting unidentified bombers. Kearby later reported about thirty-four fighters and twelve bombers.

Even with nearly twelve-to-one odds, Kearby's flight didn't hesitate. They tore into the gaggle of enemy planes, concentrating on the fighters. After several minutes of fighting and many victories, the P-47 pilots, low on ammunition, fuel, and altitude, turned toward home as the remaining Japanese planes frantically departed in the other direction.

When it was all sorted out, the Thunderbolt pilots had gotten at least nine Japanese fighters, Kearby himself dispatching six, bringing his total score to nine. The newly minted ace was later awarded the country's highest decoration for the fight—the Medal of Honor. Kearby was the first Army fighter pilot to earn the award during World War II.

Over time, another P-47 outfit, the 58th Fighter Group, arrived in the area. The 35th Fighter Group, already fighting nearby, turned in their P-38s and P-39s to become a Thunderbolt outfit. Two other units, the 9th and 36th Fighter Squadrons, also briefly flew Thunderbolts before going the other way; acquiring P-38s.

But most of the air action continued to be centered around Kearby's 348th, which tallied 326 aerial victories and produced twenty ace flyers. By late 1943, Neel Kearby had been transferred out of his fighting unit to Fifth Air Force headquarters. However, he found he was still a combat flyer at heart, often "borrowing" Thunderbolts to conduct fighter sweeps of his favorite hunting locations. By mid-January 1944, his score stood at twenty-one.

Pressure to keep pace with prolific 49th Fighter Group P-38 pilot Richard Bong—and the fact that he was nearing America's top World War I ace Eddie Rickenbacker's twenty-six kills—seemed to weigh on Kearby. He was also looked upon as the champion of the Thunderbolt, the plane that seemingly no one in the Pacific believed in. It was a great motivation to keep raising his score. These factors made his infrequent outings to Japanese hot spots all the more important.

On March 5, 1944, Kearby and two other pilots were patrolling near Wewak at twenty-two thousand feet when they observed a trio of Japanese bombers cruising at five hundred feet above the ocean. The American pilots promptly dove onto their victims, slashing down on the bombers at high speed. Two of the enemy planes were destroyed on the first pass, but Kearby's victim refused to go down. Instead of using his speed to escape into a climb, as he had preached to his flyers for months, Kearby wrenched his Thunderbolt into a tight turn and circled around to get his twenty-second kill. His bomber went down, but Kearby found himself flying at nearly stall speed and low altitude, the most vulnerable position for the big, heavy P-47.

An arriving Japanese pilot flying an Oscar took advantage of the questionable maneuver, firing into Kearby's slow-moving aircraft as he raced by. Though one of Kearby's wingmen caught and blasted the enemy pilot, the damage was already done. Pioneer P-47 ace Neel Kearby was never coming home.

THE PHILIPPINES

Slowly, the battles in the New Guinea area moved northward, with American flyers occupying airfields they had been attacking months before. Shortly after General MacArthur's return to the Philippines in late 1944, units of the Fifth Air Force moved into place, the P-47s of the 348th Fighter Group going to Leyte and the 58th Fighter Group to Mindoro.

A P-47D of the 58th Fighter Group patrols over the Philippines in 1945. The red and white-striped rudders were a "throwback" to prewar U.S. Army Air Corps markings seen in the 1930s. *National Archives*

Showing off his impressive tally of wartime victories, Major William "Dinghy" Dunham of the 348th Fighter Group poses in the cockpit of his P-47D. He ended the war with sixteen enemy fighters to his credit. *The Museum of Flight, American Fighter Aces Association*

The move north was particularly lucrative for the newly appointed commander of the 348th Fighter Group's 460th Fighter Squadron. William "Dinghy" Dunham was a veteran combat pilot with nine kills to his credit, including the Japanese flyer who had shot down Neel Kearby.

On November 18, Dunham and his flight were near Buri when they spied an American P-61 night fighter with two enemy planes in tow. As the P-47s dived, the pair escaped into a cloud. Five minutes later the two Japanese fighters (or perhaps different ones) dropped toward the Thunderbolts, and Dunham turned to meet them.

The enemy flyers must have lost their nerve, with the four sets of eight .50-calibers pointed their way, and they descended toward Cebu. Oddly, the American flyers later reported them to be an Oscar and a Mitsubishi A6M3 "Hamp" fighter. Dunham chose the Hamp as his target as his P-47 plummeted toward the mismatched pair. He closed to within thirty yards and fired away. The Hamp crashed into the water, and Dunham claimed his tenth victory.

On the third anniversary of the attack on Pearl Harbor, December 7, 1944, Dunham had the best day of his Thunderbolt-flying career. Over San Isidro Bay, he led nine other P-47s down on a group of Hamps six thousand feet below. One victim bailed out of his damaged plane as Dunham raced past. A second Hamp caught fire and crashed into the sea under the withering fire from the ace pilot's guns.

Fifteen minutes later, the American flyers couldn't believe their luck as a flight of four Oscars cruised over them, apparently not noticing the crowd of silver Jugs below. Dunham led his men into a slight climb, working his way to the enemy fighters' six o'clock position. One Japanese pilot spooked and turned away just seconds before Dunham let fly at one of the remaining three left in the formation. After a good blast of gunfire sent a bright flame spewing back from his target, he shifted his aim slightly and let another Oscar receive the last of his ammunition. Both aircraft fell into the water, and Bill Dunham's score stood at fourteen.

Right after the Thunderbolts of the 58th Fighter Group touched down at their new home on Mindoro, they were called to duty to participate in an unusual mission for the P-47: attacking enemy shipping. No bombs had arrived, so the P-47s took off with only their machine guns to attack Japanese cruisers, destroyers, and destroyer escorts that steamed close by on December 26, 1944.

Swarms of American planes—P-47s, P-40s, P-38s, and B-25s—worked frantically to repel the ships as they were shelling shore installations at Mindoro. The 58th Thunderbolts fired their guns empty and landed amidst the shelling to rearm and attack again. The damaged enemy fleet withdrew after losing one destroyer to the planes and a torpedo from an American PT boat.

In early 1945, the 348th and 58th, along with the 35th Fighter Group, were based in Luzon, at the northern end of the Philippines. Soon after, the 35th and the 348th converted to P-51 Mustangs, leaving only the 58th flying the Jug in combat in the area. By this time, much of the Japanese air forces in the area were defeated, leaving the Jugs to operate as air support for ground battles in the Philippines.

In the spring of 1945, the 58th Fighter Group was strengthened with the addition of a fourth fighter squadron. The *Escuadrón Aéreo de Pelea 201* was made up of Mexican Air Force pilots trained on the Thunderbolt within the United States. While the 58th's aircraft carried "old style" horizontal red and white-striped rudders, the Mexican aircraft flew with their nation's colors: green, white, and red, oriented vertically. The Mexican

Over Manila Bay, a Mexican pilot attached to the 201st Fighter Squadron, 58th Fighter Group, carries a load of bombs on his D-model Thunderbolt. Close inspection of the aircraft shows the Mexican national insignia on the top of the right wing as well as the green, white, and red rudder flash. *Stan Piet*

Parked at an airfield in Hangchow, China, a P-47D Thunderbolt awaits its next assignment. One wonders what the Chinese must have thought of Donald Duck and all the other characters painted on the sides of the planes. In the background is a line of P-51s assigned to the 23rd Fighter Group. *Stan Piet*

P-47s carried standard U.S. insignia on the fuselage and left upper and right lower wings, with the Mexican Air Force green, white, and red triangle on the opposite wing locations.

The foreign flyers had been trained to employ their Thunderbolts in ground-attack roles and flew 791 sorties, dropping over 350,000 pounds of bombs on enemy positions. One Mexican pilot was killed in combat before the fighting stopped. When the 201st returned to Mexico in late 1945, they left their Thunderbolts in the Pacific. The United States supplied twenty-five new P-47s to the Mexican government for continued service in North America.

CHINA, BURMA, INDIA

A fighter pilot couldn't get farther from the good old U.S.A., both literally and figuratively, than the China, Burma, India Theater (CBI) during the war years. It was a hot, humid region with mountainous jungle terrain and the most primitive flying facilities at the very end of the supply lines. In this world of extremes, the Thunderbolt's rugged construction and hearty engine were a great advantage.

P-47s that the British acquired under Lend-Lease programs served in the CBI as fighter-bombers. In late 1944, large numbers of the versatile planes were used to replace both fighters and light bombers operating in Burma. The British used their Thunderbolts primarily in the ground-attack role, supporting the British Fourteenth Army. As in the Mediterranean and Europe after D-Day, the Thunderbolts were employed to smash points of resistance for advancing armies and continually harass supply lines beyond the front.

Alongside the British Thunderbolts, a number of American groups were assigned to fly and fight the Japanese over this forbidding landscape. The 80th Fighter Group had trained in Farmingdale, New York, using Thunderbolts and then, as if traveling backwards in time, operated Curtiss P-40s and Lockheed P-38s once they stepped off their "slow boat to China" (or, actually, India). Most of the 80th transferred back to the P-47s in the spring of 1944.

Some units, such as the 33rd Fighter Group and the 81st Fighter Group, were transferred to the CBI after flying in combat in North Africa. More boisterous pilots from these units mused it was the army's cruel joke to transfer them from one "hell hole" to another without even considering places like the United Kingdom or some nice palm-covered island in the Pacific.

Originally, the army was strengthening fighter activity in the region in preparation for the arrival of B-29 heavy bombers that were slated to hit Japan from airfields in China. It was the job of the fighters in the area to keep the massive bomber airfields safe from Japanese attack. But difficulties with the regional governments, along with terrible terrain and supply problems, forced the U.S. to move its B-29 units to the Mariana Islands.

Even with the big bombers gone, some of the difficulties that chased them out of the region remained for the Thunderbolt units. Scorching heat, terrible supply problems, sickness, and seemingly endless swarms of bugs claimed more flyers than any enemy fire ever would.

Thunderbolts were used to escort the long stream of C-46 and C-47 cargo planes flying an endless supply of fuel, ammunition, food, and supplies over "the Hump" into China. Yet Japanese air activity was sparse in the region, and only a handful of Thunderbolt pilots ever caught and downed enemy planes in the CBI.

More often than not the big fighters were used to attack enemy targets on the ground in Burma. Flyers explained they often hit, but were not limited to, trains, trucks, airfields, bridges, troops, cavalry, artillery, supply dumps; and, more ruefully, trees, rocks, dirt, and crocodiles.

One pilot from the 33rd Fighter Group related an unwanted encounter with a Japanese aircraft while eight Thunderbolt pilots were doing "business as usual," concentrating on working over the enemy on the ground. During one strafing pass the commander of the flight, "Tim" Tyler, called out that the plane behind him was firing too soon; he could see tracers zipping by before he was clear of the target. Some bright flyer in the group began to count the planes in the strafing pattern, "...seven, eight, *nine!*" The unwanted visitor was a Japanese Nakajima Ki-44 Tojo fighter, happily swooping up and down, trying to get a good shot at their leader. The Tojo vacated the scene quickly once the jig was up, and the Jug pilots went home kicking themselves because they'd missed what they viewed as a golden opportunity. Tyler's crew chief counted fourteen holes in his P-47 when he landed. Angered by the events, he ordered his pilots to study aircraft recognition for weeks after the incident.

The structure of one unit that flew the Thunderbolt in the CBI was different from the rest. The 1st Air Commando Group (ACG) had been created to give support to Allied soldiers working behind Japanese lines to disrupt their operations. The flying group that supported

The landing gear of a 1st Air Commando Thunderbolt folds upwards as the plane rumbles skyward from an airfield in India. The P-47D is hauling two P-38–type fuel tanks. Many fighters operating in the CBI carried a loop-style DF antenna, used for operations over the rough terrain. *National Archives*

It's easy to forget just how young combat flyers were. A pair of Jug drivers from the 318th Fighter Group kill time before a flight from Bellows Field, Hawaii, in March 1944. *Bob Rieser via the 7th Fighter Command Association*

them, part of the Tenth Air Force, was a composite group of attack, cargo, and liaison aircraft. Each plane had distinctive diagonal stripes on the rear fuselage for instant recognition by ground and air forces.

Thunderbolts were employed with the 5th and 6th Fighter Squadrons (Commando) starting in the late summer of 1944. Before the changeover, the squadrons had been flying North American P-51A fighters. Like the other P-47 groups, these units worked primarily at hitting Japanese ground forces. On the first day of 1945, a pair of 1st ACG Thunderbolts labored into the air carrying three 1,000-pound bombs. They dropped their heavy payload on a railroad bridge. The amazing feat was successful but never repeated; it took too much fuel to carry the load effective distances. By May 1945, the squadrons had received new P-51D Mustangs and the striped Jugs were phased out of service.

HAWAII AND THE MARIANAS

The 15th Pursuit Group had been flying patrols over

Hawaii since before the attack on Pearl Harbor. In fact, on that infamous Sunday, pilots from the unit struggled into the air in Curtiss P-36 and P-40 fighters, becoming the first American airmen to do battle with the Japanese. Among the ranks of the 15th flyers that morning (though he didn't fly until the Japanese had gone) was a young lieutenant named Francis Gabreski. He soon asked to be transferred to Europe. There, he became America's leading European ace and the highest-scoring Thunderbolt flyer.

His old flying outfit, the 15th Pursuit Group, became the 15th Fighter Group, flying Bell P-39s, P-40 Warhawks, and finally receiving Thunderbolts in mid-1944. Anxious to get into combat, the 15th seemed stuck in paradise. It took another transfer to the longer-range North American P-51 Mustang to get the group into the war—they went to Iwo Jima in March 1945.

The 15th's sister outfit, the 318th Fighter Group, flew their P-47s in combat. Also based in Hawaii, the group acquired P-47s in late 1943 and received orders to

A 318th Fighter Group flyer catapults into the skies in an unusual carrier launch near Saipan in June 1944. The Thunderbolts were inserted onto the island while the battles with the Japanese defenders there were still underway. *National Archives*

proceed to the Marianas in June 1944.

Without the ability to fly to Saipan from Hawaii, the group's planes were loaded onto navy escort carriers. Their heavy Thunderbolts would be catapulted from carriers' decks once they steamed close to their new home.

One squadron nearly didn't make it. As they were nearing the launch area, the carrier USS *Manila Bay*, with its sunny flight deck filled with Thunderbolts, was refueling alongside a tanker. On the other side of the tanker, a battleship was likewise taking on fuel oil. With very little warning, a flight of Japanese Val bombers dove onto the knot of ships as they scattered, leaving the sea awash in fuel from the severed lines. But the Japanese flyers missed their big chance, their bombs falling harmlessly into the sea behind the carrier and its odd cargo.

The P-47 flyers were worried about their flight-deck takeoff, obviously a rare occurrence for an army pilot. Particularly rattled was the pilot who had a fighter with a "new, used" propeller. The sailors had quickly replaced his damaged prop with one from a Grumman TBF Avenger. "We're pretty sure it'll work just fine on the takeoff," the navy crewmen cheerfully told the less-than-confident P-47 pilot. Amazingly, it did.

They were also skeptical of the navy crew's instructions, particularly the recommendation to roll the fighter's elevator trim as far back as possible. The Thunderbolt pilots were genuinely unsure that the big Thunderbolt would fly in such a configuration. But after witnessing the first P-47s nearly brush their bellies in the water when they launched, the remaining pilots dutifully rolled their elevator trim wheels back to the stops!

At Aslito Airfield on Saipan, the pilots and their

A bare-metal P-47D of the 318th Fighter Group is photographed by a curious soldier on Saipan. The army often used the planes to attack targets on the island and its nearby neighbor, Tinian. When the planes were bombing Tinian, the group's ground crew could sometimes see their pilots in action from the airfield on Saipan. *National Museum of the United States Air Force*

crews found that the ground fighting was far from over. They went about creating their camp and flight line amidst constant threat of attack and a steady drizzle of sniper's bullets.

Anxious to get into the fighting, the 318th Fighter Group Thunderbolt pilots almost immediately began flying combat air patrols against Japanese air threats and close-air-support and ground attacks on Saipan and the neighboring islands.

For ground attacks, the Thunderbolts employed 500-pound bombs (as well as "returning" a few captured Japanese bombs), fired rocket tubes, and dropped fuel tanks filled with napalm. The jellied gasoline in particu-

Near Saipan, a P-47D of the 318th Fighter Group patrols the skies. Pilots say the planes were getting a little long in the tooth by the time they were committed to combat—this one has a replacement canopy. Later, the 318th moved forward to Ie Shima and received new P-47Ns. *7th Fighter Command Association*

Working well into the night, ground crewmen load a raft into the left pylon of a 318th Fighter Group Thunderbolt on Saipan. After the bulk of the fighting in the area was over, the Thunderbolts were used for defensive patrols and scouting for lost American bombers. *National Archives*

The old and new. On the flight line in New York sits a late model P-47D (left) and the XP-47N. The squared-off wings of the latter are immediately noticeable. Closer study reveals that the N-model's overall wingspan is thirty-six inches more; an eighteen-inch section added on either side near the wing root gave the new-version Thunderbolt room to carry more internal fuel. *National Archives*

lar was damaging to the morale of the Japanese and equally uplifting to the 318th's ground crews, who could watch their flyers' strikes on nearby Tinian Island from their own airfield on Saipan.

The 318th's fighting radius slowly widened as the Japanese army and air threats were eliminated—Saipan, Tinian, Rota, Pagan, and Guam. By fall of 1944, huge B-29s were coming into the Marianas bases, and the P-47 fighters had driven out almost all Japanese air resistance within range.

With their P-47s loaded to the gills with fuel, the 318th flyers tried to spring an attack on Japanese fighters that often followed American bombers on their return trip from attacking Iwo Jima. The Thunderbolts couldn't make it the whole way, but the pilots figured they could briefly tangle with any Zeros who ranged too far south while harassing the Marianas-based B-24s. Their trap, after hours and hours in the air, snared only a solitary Japanese Kawasaki Ki-45 Nick twin-engine fighter.

Their base was quickly becoming a backwater, and their P-47s were only good for defense of the B-29 bases growing in the Marianas. The group briefly brought in some longer-range P-38s "borrowed" from a Hawaii-

based fighter outfit to reach Iwo Jima, but most pilots of the 318th would have to cool their heels doing endless combat air patrols until they were moved closer to Japan.

OKINAWA AND IE SHIMA

The 318th's problems were solved when they received new P-47N Thunderbolts and were ordered to prepare

A P-47N-1-RE dubbed *The Repulsive Thunder Box* cruises over the United States late in the war. *National Archives*

Model:	P-47N-1-RE		**Empty Weight:**	10,988 pounds
Number Built:	550		**Gross Weight:**	13,823 pounds
Engine:	Pratt & Whitney R-2800-57		**Maximum Weight:**	21,200 pounds
Power Rating:	2,100/2,800 hp			
Propeller:	Curtiss Electric, 13 feet diameter		**Maximum Speed:**	467 mph at 32,000 feet
			Landing Speed:	98 mph
			Service Ceiling:	43,000 feet
Span:	42 feet 6.56 inches		**Internal Fuel:**	556 gallons
Length:	36 feet 1.75 inches		**Maximum Range:**	2,000 miles at 25,000 feet
Height:	14 feet 6 inches			
Wing Area:	322.2 square feet		**Armament:**	8 x .50-caliber machine guns, 267 to 500 rounds per gun 3 x 1,000-pound bombs

to move forward. They were going to Ie Shima, a small island near Okinawa. Just 325 miles from Japan, they could now range over the Japanese home islands in their new Thunderbolts and loiter in enemy airspace for long durations. Veterans of the fight on Saipan, the 318th's men weren't even overly nervous about their return to the front lines and primitive living conditions.

What did bother them when they arrived in late April 1945 was the size of the airfield they had been assigned. The field on "Peanut Island," as the airmen sometimes called Ie Shima, would have been perfect for Stinson liaison planes but was dangerously undersized for their monstrous ten-ton N-model Thunderbolts when loaded with fuel, bombs, rockets, and ammunition. They wanted at least 5,800 feet under dry conditions. What they received was 3,700 feet of sticky coral and sloppy mud under usually hot and dreary skies. If pilots could wrench the stick back far enough to clear a rocky embankment at the end of the field, it was a four-

hundred-foot drop to the sea. They used the fall to gain a little airspeed before pulling away, often leaving an ocean-spray wake with their propellers. Flyers used every trick in the book to get their P-47Ns hopping: taking advantage of sometimes more than every inch of runway, full power, full turbo, water injection, a small dose of flaps, and a large helping of prayer.

A Republic representative visiting the island was skeptical of the pilot's complaints. He said that they were wasting too much fuel during these all-out takeoffs through the flyers' selection of too high manifold boost. It could be done with less, the tech rep claimed, and he'd show them how.

In a fully loaded P-47N, he began his takeoff roll. By the time he reached the crest of the incline that marked roughly the halfway point of the runway, the pilots watching feared that the Republic pilot was going too slow to make it. But at that point, he was committed. The tail wheel of the Thunderbolt slowly rose from the

coral strip, and in the last few feet of runway, the pilot fought to make the heavy fighter fly. The tail hit the ground with a horrible thump as the plane mushed into the rocks beyond the field, bursting into a gasoline-fueled inferno. The Republic pilot's death only reinforced what the flyers already knew: operating their loaded P-47s from Ie Shima's short field was an exceedingly dangerous game.

Those who managed to "dice with death" and win took on a number of different duties once flying. Ie Shima's close proximity to active Japanese air bases made it a lucrative target for *kamikaze* flights, and the Thunderbolts of the 318th Fighter Group, as well as fellow P-47N units, the 413th Fighter Group (which arrived in May) and the 507th (which arrived in June) took turns defending the Okinawa area from attack.

Others, much to their chagrin, were chosen to fly to Japan at night to harass air bases and other targets. Ill-equipped for the task, the night missions were truly "white-knuckle affairs" from takeoff to (hopefully) landing, with a good bit of stumbling around in the dark in between. The pilots mostly used the rockets and ammunition they brought along in attempts to signal one another when lost in the inky darkness, as opposed to

hitting anything important in enemy territory.

But the job the Thunderbolt flyers liked best, of course, was air-fighting. And over Japan at this late stage in the war, the enemy pilots they encountered were more

often than not fairly new to the air combat game, which resulted in exceedingly good hunting.

On May 25, two P-47 pilots of the 318th, Lt. Richard Anderson and Lt. Don Kennedy, were flying near Amami O Shima when they spotted a group of thirty planes headed for Okinawa. At first, they figured they were marine Corsair fighters, but as they got closer, they saw the planes were Japanese Zeke fighters.

Despite the odds, the pair rammed their throttles forward and tore into the pack of Zeros. The Japanese pilots were fairly inexperienced, tasked with a one-way trip to crash into American ships near Okinawa. They did little to outmaneuver the attacking P-47s or cover one another from the eager American pilots. When it was over, Anderson had flamed five Zekes and Kennedy had bagged three. Anderson, who became an ace-in-a-day, was blasting away at his sixth victim when he ran out of ammunition.

Three days later, Capt. John Vogt shot down five Zekes over Kanoya in southern Kyushu. In all, the 318th group P-47s shot down seventeen enemy fighters that day without losing any of their number in combat. The news wasn't all good, however; two flyers had to skip the mission, jettisoning their fuel tanks in "hairy" takeoffs. Another pilot had been killed when his P-47 crashed at the end of one of Ie Shima's shoddy runways.

In June, the 318th continued to press their attacks and met with some amazing successes. On June 6, Capt. Judge Wolfe shot down a pair of Zekes, the first of which he hit with a barrage of rockets while lightening up his aircraft to fight. Wolfe and his flyers encountered a formation of seven Japanese fighters on June 10, and the formation blasted every one of the enemy planes before their pilots knew what hit them.

But the "star" of the day was Lt. Robert Stone, a member of Wolfe's execution squad who got two planes in the short fight. He became separated from the others and was running for his life at treetop level over Kyushu with a pair of Zekes nipping at his tail. His speeding path led him over an airbase, where he narrowly missed a Betty bomber on final approach. His pursuers were not as lucky: the three planes collided in a fiery mess, crashing to the ground. Amazingly, Stone is credited with the destruction of a total of five Japanese planes for the mission, only two of which he had actually fired upon.

Fittingly, the last P-47 group to Ie Shima, the 507th, produced World War II's last ace on one of the last days of the war. Both atomic bombs had been dropped and the Soviets had begun to push the Japanese out of Manchuria when Lt. Oscar Perdomo and thirty-seven other Thunderbolt pilots made a long-range fighter sweep over Keijo (Seoul), Korea, on August 13. Perdomo bagged four formidable Ki-84 Frank fighters and some poor Japanese airman who strayed into the combat zone flying a trainer plane. Perdomo's gun camera footage showed the big Jug's eight .50-calibers absolutely shredding the small wood and fabric biplane.

IWO JIMA

While the 507th Fighter Group produced the last ace, they were not the last to begin their wartime combat service. That distinction goes to the 414th Fighter Group, flying their P-47Ns from Iwo Jima. By the time they arrived on the remote, desolate island in late July 1945, it was a hopping American airbase, with day and night fighters and an emergency field for Boeing B-29 heavy bombers.

Pilots puzzled over their assignment. While the other P-47N groups went to Ie Shima (except for the 508th Fighter Group, which never moved farther than Hawaii), the 414th had landed on Iwo, which was about twice the distance from the Japanese home islands as Ie Shima. The flyers quickly did range experiments to see how the Thunderbolt would perform over the 750-mile trip to the action.

P-47Ns took off with two 165-gallon tanks, a 108-gallon centerline tank, six rockets, and 3,200 rounds of ammunition on July 29. Flying relatively near home, they stayed aloft for ten hours, plenty of time to make a VLR (very long range) attack on Japan. The next day, they took off with the same load, but with a 500-pound bomb in the place of the center fuel tank. The results were not as good: six and a half hours. Their attacks on Japan would have to be with rockets and machine guns only, no bombs.

The vast increase in range with the P-47N was amazing. When Kearby's Thunderbolts arrived in the Pacific in mid-1943, his planes could go 200 miles on internal fuel and perhaps 320 with his Australian external tanks. Flying from Iwo Jima, aircraft of the 414th flew more than 1,400 miles on round trips to Japan.

Another inevitable comparison came right away. The island of Iwo Jima was teeming with North American P-51D Mustangs, three fighter groups worth of them, and the Thunderbolt pilots promptly initiated mock dogfights with their counterparts. In a fight, the Mustang was king, outclassing the performance of the P-47N in almost every way except the Jug's amazing ability to dive.

However, the Thunderbolt pilots were quick to point out the practical advantages of their mount. At this stage in the fighting, there weren't going to be many all-out air-to-air tussles over the Japanese Empire. And, the P-47 had more guns for ground attack; a hearty, air-cooled engine that was less susceptible to battle damage; and a notoriously roomy cockpit (with autopilot) for the long flights over the Pacific.

After a few local attacks to Japanese-held islands around Iwo Jima, the 414th headed to Japan on August 1, pounding two airfields and returning to Iwo after nearly ten hours in the air. They completed only two additional VLR missions before the war's end. According to the group's historian, the final one, on August 14, was called a "persuader" mission; it was known that Japan would soon surrender, "but it became apparent they were taking too much time." Sadly, one pilot from the group was forced to bail out when hit by antiaircraft fire. When he jumped from his stricken P-47, he struck the tail of his aircraft. Picked up by a rescue submarine, the flyer died from his injuries in the final hours of World War II.

Iwo Jima's aircraft, including the P-47s of the 414th, made one final flight to Japan in late August as part of a "show of power" over General Douglas MacArthur's arrival at Atsugi Airfield outside of Tokyo. The group's history recounted how "tremendous B-29 formations droned overhead as navy fighters darted about over hundreds of warships in Tokyo Bay participating in landing operations. Air power was overwhelming, and the Field Day complete."

After traveling halfway around the globe, a new P-47N Thunderbolt sits at an airfield on Guam, awaiting a relatively short flight to its final destination—Ie Shima or Iwo Jima. Even with their increased range, the fighters were brought into the Pacific on ships. *Harold Gronenthal via 7th Fighter Command Association*

It was a sad sight for Jug drivers when combat-veteran P-47s deemed too weary or old to be shipped home were destroyed on the spot. The fighters were cut apart and fed into smelters to make new aluminum ingots for the recovering German economy. *National Archives*

The Territory of Hawaii's Air National Guard was the last American unit to operate the Thunderbolt. Here, an N-model Jug is photographed with a North American F-86 Sabre fighter and a Lockheed T-33 two-seat jet trainer. *The Museum of Flight, Taylor collection*

CHAPTER EIGHT

STILL FLYING: P-47s AFTER WORLD WAR II

A large number of P-47 Thunderbolts survived World War II intact. For a time, the army operated the fighters in the United States and in combat-ready units abroad. Still later, the United States Air National Guard patrolled vast sections of America with the venerable Jug, as did many of the nation's allies in the first years of the Cold War. In a few out-of-the-way hot spots, a handful of Thunderbolts would engage in battle again.

AT WAR'S END

When the fighting in Europe ceased, there were nearly six thousand Thunderbolts flying from airfields in France, Britain, Italy, and Germany. Many of these aircraft were transferred to an airfield in Speke, England, near the port of Liverpool in preparation for a new mission. These were largely the most modern or newest examples in theater, some of which were fresh from the factory, with very little flying time.

Speke's Thunderbolts were destined to return to the United States via cargo ship, for overhaul before being delivered to the Pacific. Some believed the war with Japan could go on for another year or more. Valuable fighters like the P-47 and P-51 Mustang were slated to participate in battles to push the Japanese out of China or perhaps a costly invasion of Japan's home islands.

The blasts of two atomic bombs and Japan's surrender in August 1945 changed the army's plans. While aircraft were no longer urgently needed in the Pacific, the troublesome task of bringing airplanes, equipment, vehicles, and personnel home from all over the globe was daunting enough.

The army wanted to retain large portions of its aircraft fleet for postwar services and to equip allies throughout the world. The top aircraft types were B-29 and B-17 heavy bombers, B-25 and A-26 medium bombers, C-47 cargo planes, and P-51 and P-47 fighter aircraft. These types were flown or shipped to America in large numbers.

Again, there were exceptions. Massive collections of aircraft allowed officials to pick and choose, condemning many a battle-scarred veteran airframe to death. In Europe, faded and battered Thunderbolts were chopped or blasted into pieces and fed into smelters, creating fresh aluminum ingots for local rebuilding efforts. One P-47 flyer wrote that he watched them blow up their "beautiful

Packed onto an airfield at Speke, England, Thunderbolts with less than one hundred combat hours were readied for transport to the Pacific after the end of war in Europe. Luckily, they weren't needed. *National Archives*

airplanes" in Austria. "They took a Vultee Vengeance bomber and loaded it with twenty-five pounds of dynamite and completely destroyed it. A Martin B-26 was next, and seventy-five pounds of TNT ripped it apart. Then they put a P-47 on blocks and loaded it with one hundred pounds and set it off," he wrote. "It merely blew the inspection plates off. And that story is not far from the truth."

In the remote Pacific, there were fewer locals to benefit from the recycled plane parts. Usually, commanders simply ordered old Jugs to be bulldozed, buried, pushed into a jungle ravine, or dropped into the sea.

A few select fighter groups continued to operate in and around Axis nations as part of the Allies' occupying forces. For example, Korean War ace Frederick "Boots" Blesse began his operational flying career with an Okinawa-based P-47 fighter squadron in 1946 and 1947. He recalls that flying the Thunderbolts, which had been put into temporary storage in the Pacific since the war's end, was a "harem, scarem existence." Many of the planes had faulty rubber hoses and suspect fuel lines, leading to much excitement on many flights.

Many Thunderbolts shipped back to the United States arrived at Tinker army airfield in Oklahoma. The country's largest repair and maintenance depot featured massive parking areas with row after row of P-47s awaiting overhaul and reassignment or disposal.

THE AIR NATIONAL GUARD
Most Thunderbolts were phased out of active duty with the AAF soon after World War II. However, the aviation arm of the National Guard retained the venerable Jugs, along with loads of P-51 Mustang fighters. In rough

After the war, hundreds of Thunderbolts were packed into long lines at Oklahoma's Tinker Air Force Base. The neat rows were jumbled by two tornadoes that touched down at the airfield in March 1948. *Oklahoma City Air Logistics Center Office of History*

In 1949, American occupation troops staged large-scale maneuvers in northern Bavaria to test how fast they could repel an attack from communist forces. As they had years before, Thunderbolts worked closely with ground forces in coordinated attacks. *National Archives*

A P-47N of the Delaware Air National Guard patrols snow-topped mountains of Wyoming in 1949. The unit received the Thunderbolts in late 1946. The dual antenna near the tail is an "Uncle Dog" radio direction finder, installed on many fighter aircraft stationed in the Pacific during World War II. *The Museum of Flight, Taylor collection*

You could fly a Thunderbolt through a brick wall and live, pilots claimed. After a messy tangle with an airfield out-building, this Maryland Air National Guard F-47 looked as if it was still in pretty good shape! *The Museum of Flight, Taylor collection*

terms, P-51s populated the fighter squadrons in the West and Midwest, while Thunderbolts flew in the East, parts of the South, and the territories of Hawaii and Puerto Rico. The Air National Guard (ANG) Thunderbolts were late-model P-47Ds and P-47Ns.

The first Thunderbolt arrived at Connecticut's 118th Fighter Squadron at Windsor Locks in the last part of 1946. By all accounts, guard pilots were as fond of the Thunderbolts as World War II combat flyers had been. The P-47 had proven to be incredibly tough and dependable, characteristics that transcended wartime service.

There were rumors of a Georgia ANG pilot who undershot his landing, plowing his Jug through the second story of a brick factory building. The plane's wings tore off as the fuselage torpedoed through the rooms. Supposedly, the pilot climbed from the crushed cockpit and walked away with only a bump on the head.

In 1947, the United States Army Air Forces became a separate military branch, the United States Air Force. And in 1948, the remaining P-47s became F-47 Thunderbolts, the *pursuit* designation replaced with the *fighter* prefix.

When North Korean forces pushed across the 38th parallel in June 1950, the United States and its aircraft were thrown into the fighting. Though jets were firmly established as the future of air power, the nature of the fighting in Korea compelled air force officials to continue to rely on a sizable force of piston-engine planes, many of them World War II vintage.

For the role of fighter-bomber, squadrons flying the North American F-51 Mustang were sent overseas. The choice of the Mustang has caused many to wonder why the USAF passed over the Thunderbolt, proven to be an

The combat veteran 352nd Fighter Group flew Mustangs as part of the Eighth Air Force during the war. The unit was retired briefly and then reactivated, flying Thunderbolts as the 113th Fighter Group of the District of Columbia Air National Guard in 1946. Their motto was *Custodes pro Defensione* (Guardians for Defense). *The Museum of Flight, Taylor collection*

exceptional fighter-bomber. It was more heavily armed, could carry more ordnance, and was more survivable than the F-51. The Mustang's Achilles heel was its liquid-cooling system, especially vulnerable to ground fire—and there was plenty of ground fire at the altitude and areas in which the F-51s were working in Korea.

F-51s were most likely chosen because more were available, serving in active air force squadrons, some of which were deployed overseas. Air force brass viewed the Mustang as the better overall aircraft, slated to be in service for years to come.

There were about 350 F-47 Thunderbolts in fighting shape in 1950, and almost every one was in the ANG. Perhaps 150 more were in dusty storage depots in various states of disrepair. While the Thunderbolt might have been better for the job at hand, supporting it would have been a more difficult proposition.

Still, F-51 losses in the skies over Korea were quite high—higher than those of the jet-powered Lockheed F-80s and Republic F-84s fighting there. At one point in 1951, the commander of the United States' Far East Air Forces, Lt. Gen. George Edward Stratemeyer, requested that F-47s in the United States replace the F-51s lost. Air Force Chief of Staff Gen. Hoyt Vandenberg told Stratemeyer to forget about introducing a second obsolete aircraft type to Korea, and the issue was dropped.

The drain on fighters did affect units within the

Two of Long Island's most famous fighters fly in formation over their home. During World War II, Republic made over 15,600 Thunderbolts, while just a few miles to the west, Grumman Aircraft Engineering Corporation churned out more than 12,200 F6F Hellcat navy fighters. *The Museum of Flight*

United States. Some jet squadrons were switched back to F-51s. Some F-51 squadrons stepped in to relieve jet units transferred overseas. And three ANG squadrons operating F-47 Thunderbolts were called back into active service in 1951 and 1952: the 141st of New Jersey, 149th of Virginia, and 153rd of Mississippi. But no Thunderbolt fired a shot as America's air forces

A P-47D of the North Carolina Air National Guard, decked out in a fictional paint scheme for the movie *Fighter Squadron*, in Marietta, Georgia, in 1946. *The Museum of Flight, Taylor collection*

fought in Asia.

The last air force unit to operate the F-47 Thunderbolt was the Territory of Hawaii ANG's 199th Fighter Intercept Squadron, which switched to jet aircraft in 1954. As it turned out, after V-E Day, U. S. Thunderbolts never again saw combat, but P-47s/F-47s that America's allies acquired participated in postwar scraps throughout the world.

THUNDERBOLTS IN FOREIGN SERVICE

Mexico, Britain, Russia, France, and Brazil operated P-47s during World War II. As the United States continued to develop new types of frontline aircraft, many more countries acquired the Thunderbolt for use in their postwar air forces. P-47s, and later F-47s, touched down in a long list of countries all around the world—France, Nationalist China, Portugal, the former Yugoslavia, Iran, Mexico, Turkey, and Italy. Many others went south, to Central and South American countries—Bolivia, Brazil, Chile, Colombia, Dominica, Ecuador, Guatemala, Honduras, Nicaragua, Peru, and Venezuela. A handful of other Thunderbolts are rumored to have escaped official channels and ended up elsewhere—Haiti, Cuba, Communist China, and Argentina. In a number of areas, the shooting war didn't stop with the end of World War II, and throughout the late 1940s and 1950s, foreign Thunderbolts took part in the action.

CHINA

On November 1, 1952, the U.S. Navy escort carrier USS *Windham Bay* arrived in Kaohsiung Harbor in Taiwan. On the deck was a mass of F-47N Thunderbolts encased in protective gray coating to shield them from the salt air. Members of the air force from the Republic of China inspected each of the machines as they were lifted off the deck.

As the Korean War moved toward its conclusion, newly elected President Dwight D. Eisenhower lifted the U.S. military blockade on the Strait of Taiwan, thus

Generally, Republic Thunderbolts, like this Maryland Air National Guard F-47D, were used to fill ANG fighter units in the East and parts of the South after the war. At the same time, F-51 Mustangs populated units in the West and Midwest. *Stan Piet*

As jet fighters came into service in the late 1950s, Colombia disposed of its Thunderbolts by pushing them into a river. This P-47D, outside an air museum facility in 1974, is the only survivor. *The Museum of Flight, Taylor collection*

allowing a fragile peace between the Nationalist Chinese (those evacuated to Taiwan during the Chinese civil war) and the People's Republic of China (the Communist forces of mainland China) to come to an end.

The newly acquired F-47N Thunderbolts were the most advanced aircraft ever supplied to America's ally, the Nationalist Chinese. The new planes allowed some World War II-era fighters, including a number of older P-47Ds, to be transferred from frontline service to training units.

The Nationalists had wanted jets. Communist China had Soviet-built MiG-15s on the prowl in the skies over the mainland, seemingly at a great advantage when matched up against the prop-driven Jugs from the last war. In fact, by 1953 the United States was helping the Nationalists step into the jet age, supplying Lockheed T-33 trainers and a number of Republic F-84G fighters. But learning to fly advanced weaponry would take time. The general principles and tactics used in the employment of prop-driven aircraft in combat were familiar to many Nationalist pilots—veterans of the fighting with Communist China and, previously, the Japanese.

The F-47Ns were moved north to bases within striking range of mainland China, and the first combat mission flown by the aircraft took place on July 25, 1953. The pilots chosen for this inaugural flight were 1st Lt. Lo Fu-Jer, the lead pilot, and 2nd Lt. Tien Shi-San, his wing-

The Chinese received many of the Thunderbolts operating in the CBI after the war was over. This P-47D looks like it once belonged to the 81st Fighter Group before being turned over to its new owners. Note the blacked-out shape of an American national insignia with the Chinese white and blue sunburst painted over the top. *Stan Piet*

man. The pair took off that morning for the coast of mainland China, looking for targets of opportunity. On the way, Tien's aircraft developed a slight oil leak that turned progressively worse after the flyers departed their target area, not having found anything worthwhile to attack. Suddenly, two MiG-15s jumped the F-47Ns. While

A Soviet-built MiG-15 fighter moments after takeoff—in the hands of pilots from the People's Republic of China, the jets were more than a handful for Nationalist Chinese flyers operating surplus F-47Ns. *The Museum of Flight*

Lo escaped, the MiGs made repeated attacks on Tien, who evaded them by throttling back, flying at low level, and maneuvering violently. Parrying with the MiGs and struggling to see through an oil-splattered canopy, he made it back to Taiwan. During his landing roll, the F-47's engine quit, starved of fuel. Young Tien Shi-San became a hero among the Nationalist Chinese pilots, and was asked to lecture about his tactics, developed "on the fly" to defeat the MiGs' firing runs. Over the next few months, the F-47s went back into battle, attacking ground and shipping targets with bombs and guns. During these missions, F-47s again tangled with MiGs. Sometimes the MiGs got their prey. Amazingly, in other encounters, Thunderbolts are reported to have shot down the advanced jets with their .50-calibers. Over time, the aging F-47Ns were phased out in favor of jets acquired from the United States.

FRANCE
Right after World War II ended, France became involved in battles to reclaim French Indochina (Vietnam). Initially, French air force personnel were using any aircraft

French Thunderbolts fly in formation over Algeria. The fighter-bombers lugged bombs in support of French ground troops. *The Museum of Flight, Bowers collection*

they could find, including abandoned Japanese planes. Thunderbolts were needed in the fighter-bomber role, but difficulties prevented their deployment. The United States was not particularly supportive of France's endeavors in the Far East and refused to commit to supplying the spare parts necessary to keep the French Jugs flying in combat. Also, nearly every airfield in Indochina was not long or sturdy enough to accommodate loaded Thunderbolts.

Beginning in 1954, the United States was more supportive of France's actions in the North African colony of Algeria, when the French air force introduced F-47s to the area. Though the *Escadre de Chasse 20* was considered an advanced training unit, "training" included using their Thunderbolts for close air support duties. French pilot Claude Périlhon wrote that he found it easy to join an F-47 squadron because most flyers believed it to be suicide. He says there was little in the way of actual training, because it was viewed as a waste of the limited amount of time left on the old P-47 airframe, time better devoted to fighting.

Périlhon related that the big, bruising Thunderbolts were often called in to the roughest battles—situations for which smaller, armed North American T-6 aircraft were insufficient. The aging F-47s were considered "heavy lifters," carrying more rockets, bombs, and ammunition.

There were generally more pilots than Thunderbolts. The planes were often in use from sunup to sundown. The F-47s mostly supported French ground units, hitting concentrations of Algerian nationalists.

The planes worked in pairs, arriving at fifteen thousand feet. A spotter in a small Piper scout plane would fire a smoke rocket near the target and give directions to the aim point. Périlhon wrote that the Piper pilots would radio directions, often forgetting that "a few meters to the left" or "just a hair to the right" meant nothing to the Jug pilots orbiting at fifteen thousand feet. He related that they could hardly ever even *see* the small spotter plane from their perch.

When the Piper pilots had thoroughly apprised the F-47 flyers of the situation—including good directions on where the enemy and friendly units were located—they would roll into their dives, commonly taking fire from five thousand feet to "three feet from the ground." They flew quite low to drop their bombs, trying to avoid French soldiers nearby. The Thunderbolts often carried bombs with eleven-second delayed fuses.

Like others who flew the Thunderbolt in combat, the French airmen marveled at the durability and toughness of their old fighters. Algeria's sand didn't seem to bother the planes, and the constant smattering of gunfire caused difficulties only on rare occasions. The pilots soon adopted the nickname "Flying Bulldozer" for the F-47, as their American counterparts had before them.

There were also the standard complaints: for example, the Thunderbolt took forever to take off and to climb, especially when it was hot. Just for fun, they tangled with French navy Corsairs. "It was the Corsair that led the dance," pilots recalled.

In essence, the Thunderbolts were used up in combat, through both battle damage and heavy use. They were eventually replaced by other types of warplanes, including surplus Douglas Skyraiders. After years of fighting, Algeria became an independent nation in 1962, and the French withdrew their forces.

LATIN AMERICA

Perhaps the strangest story of Thunderbolt postwar combat comes from Latin America. In 1950, the election of Jacobo Arbenz Guzmán as president of Guatemala did not sit well with many American leaders. As far as they were concerned, Arbenz was a communist. Perhaps closer to the truth, Guatemala's new man was interested in limiting the power of an American-controlled multinational corporation, the United Fruit Company.

To "contain communism," the CIA moved aircraft through a front company to the area in 1953. A potpourri of winged machines, including six F-47Ns, were "loaned" to the CIA by the Puerto Rican Air National Guard and then rented to Nicaragua for one dollar each. But the planes weren't flown by Nicaraguan pilots; the CIA had gathered an oddball collection of mercenaries to fly missions over Guatemala. Among them was Jerry DeLarm, a World War II combat pilot who had been living down south for many years.

The work of overthrowing Arbenz began in January 1954, when opposition forces dropped leaflets demanding his ouster and warning that rebels would come. These forces, led by CIA-designated leader-to-be Carlos Castillo Armas, began their takeover attempts in June. Two unmarked F-47s dropped small fragmentation bombs, distributed leaflets, and blasted the national palace.

To create the illusion of a large armada of aircraft, the attacks over the next few days included C-47s, AT-6s, a Cessna 180, and the Thunderbolts. Flying the Cessna, DeLarm and another flyer reportedly dropped a grenade and a stick of dynamite out the cabin windows onto a fuel storage tank in an attempt to set it afire.

The Thunderbolts of the ragtag air force were often damaged by ground fire, and the United States released two F-51D Mustangs to make up for the losses. The CIA forces were having the desired effect on Arbenz's government—sowing panic and paranoia.

The new junta, led by Castillo Armas, took over on July 1, 1954. Nicaragua acquired three of the remaining F-47s, while one remained in Guatemala. DeLarm used the latter to strafe army troops unhappy with the country's new government. This plane, along with DeLarm's services, was later transferred to Nicaragua.

In early 1955, the well-used Thunderbolts were in use again, this time in an attempt by Nicaragua to invade parts of Costa Rica. The defending country appealed to the United States for (what else?) Thunderbolts to counter the threat. They received four F-51Ds.

Before the invasion was repelled, one of the American-supplied Mustangs was lost and the pilot killed. Investigation found a number of heavy-caliber bullets in the mangled fighter's hide. Some believe that DeLarm and his Thunderbolt ambushed the ill-trained Costa Rican airman—perhaps a strange case of two World War II brothers fighting it out over Central American skies.

SURVIVING P-47s

Only a few P-47 Thunderbolts produced during America's great years of war production survive today. Fewer than 60 of the more than 15,600 aircraft from assembly lines are known to exist, less than 0.4 percent. By comparison, around 280, nearly 2 percent, of the more than 14,800 North American P-51 Mustangs are still flying or on display in museums. Similar to the Mustang, the Thunderbolt's post-war service spread planes all over, with rare surviving examples located across the globe, in

At the Cradle of Aviation Museum in Long Island, New York, a Republic P-47N is exhibited among the other famous aircraft built and flown in the region. The aircraft is on loan from the National Museum of the United States Air Force in Dayton, Ohio. *Author's collection*

The Reynolds Bombshell was a P-47M found in a Recon-struction Finance Corporation yard in 1946. The plane, sponsored by Milton Reynolds and Dallas Aero Services, was entered into the Los Angeles-to-Cleveland Bendix Trophy Race in 1947. To make the nonstop trip, the Thunderbolt was fitted with drop tanks. Fuel leaks kept the unique fighter from ever participat-ing in the race. *The Museum of Flight, Taylor collection*

In Seattle, an ex-Bolivian Thunderbolt is displayed in a gallery filled with World War II fighters at The Museum of Flight. The razorback P-47D wears the scheme of Lt. Col. Robert Baseler's 325th Fighter Group aircraft. *Bill Mohn*

Outside the Confederate Air Force's national headquarters hangar at Rebel Field in Texas, two of Ed Jurist's six ex-Peruvian Thunderbolts were photographed after restoration. *The Museum of Flight, Taylor collection*

the former Yugoslavia, China, the United Kingdom, Australia, France, Turkey, Italy, and a handful in South and Central America.

Most P-47 survivors are located in the United States, but many of them were recovered after stints serving with Latin American nations. The Museum of Flight's example in Seattle is from Bolivia. The Jug at the Lone Star Flight Museum in Galveston is from Venezuela. By the time the P-47 emerged as a rare warbird worth salvation, examples had been nearly eradicated from the United States.

Collectors were obliged to head south to see what languished on the sides of jungle airstrips or stood on a pole at the gates of a banana republic air force base. And if this endeavor could be considered a contest, ex-WWII pilot and aviation enthusiast Ed Jurist is the hands-down winner. In a single deal, he bought six P-47Ds and a mountain of spare parts from the Peruvian air force in 1967.

The caper was anything but easy. The expected gouging from various officials was the least of Jurist's worries when he fell ill and then was not permitted to leave the country. It took attorneys, doctors, and Jurist's wife to wrangle a spot for him on an outbound passen-

ger plane. The determined salvage hunter was not finished with the mission, but he was wise enough to continue his arrangements from the United States.

It took him until the fall of 1969 to obtain permits and make arrangements to get the parts, pieces, and dismantled planes onto a northbound ship, the *Rosaldina*. During the trip, the *Rosaldina* disappeared as a hurricane hit the Gulf of Mexico. Jurist must have felt he was cursed. But after the storm, the ship was discovered safely tucked into a harbor. Finally, the vessel and its priceless cargo arrived in Brownsville, Texas.

All six P-47s were restored to flying condition. Each received a paint job of a different WWII fighter group. Jurist sold the Thunderbolts, plus other planes, to restaurateur David Tallichet in 1975. The collection was later split apart. At one time, the results of Jurist's Peruvian aircraft adventure were on display at the Palm Springs Air Museum in California, the National Museum of the United States Air Force in Ohio, the Kalamazoo Air Zoo in Michigan, the Fighter Collection in Duxford, England, and in the hands of collectors in Nevada and Illinois.

A year after the sale to Tallichet, a long saga began near the nation's capitol that would prove to be many a

Painted as a 353rd Fighter Group Thunderbolt, this P-47D was one of the aircraft Ed Jurist recovered from Peru. Today this plane is on display at the National Museum of the United States Air Force. *The Museum of Flight, Taylor collection*

Jug pilot's last fight. The opening of the Smithsonian Institution's National Air and Space Museum (NASM) main hall was a great occasion for celebration in 1976. However, after the fanfare had subsided, many ex-Thunderbolt pilots were disappointed to find that Gallery 205, the World War II aviation display, lacked their beloved aircraft. In fact, when the P-47 Thunderbolt Pilots Association began sending letters to NASM president Michael Collins in 1977, they requested that the Smithsonian obtain a Thunderbolt. There was even talk about raising money to acquire a Jug for the museum. If they could have located one, the asking price would have been about $120,000 in those days.

But the Smithsonian had acquired an example of the Jug years before. Serial number 44-32691 had been used as a gunnery trainer on the East Coast during the war and had been transferred to the U.S. Army Air Forces Museum in 1946. After the Smithsonian acquired the plane in 1965, it lent it to Republic Aviation for restoration and display for the twentieth anniversary of P-47's first flight. Once returned to the Washington area, the big fighter was stored at the Paul Garber Facility in Suitland, Maryland.

When the P-47 Thunderbolt Pilots Association members found that the Smithsonian indeed possessed a P-47, they seemed to "flip on their gun sights and run up the RPMs," looking for a fight. Strafing museum officials with letters, they asked, "Why should planes operated by enemy combatants have permanent spots in this nation's gallery while the Thunderbolt sits unwanted in a dusty restoration facility?"

NASM's World War II gallery contained a German Messerschmitt Bf-109, British Supermarine Spitfire, Japanese A6M Zero, Italian Macchi C.202, and a North American P-51 Mustang. Other WWII-era aircraft were displayed in other parts of the building as well: a Wildcat and Dauntless navy aircraft in the air-sea operations area, a Messerschmitt Me-262 and Lockheed P-80 in the jet aviation gallery, and a Curtiss P-40 hanging in the west gallery.

The blow-by-blow correspondence to and from various Smithsonian leaders appeared in nearly every issue of the Thunderbolt Pilot's Association *Jug Letter* for years. There are requests signed by some of the most prominent Thunderbolt aces, threats to withhold donations, debates about the size and hanging weight of the Jug, and the overriding opinion that "those foreign" aircraft that were so often fodder for the Jug's eight .50-calibers should be moved out of the *national* museum, or at least rotated yearly, to make room for a permanent display for the Thunderbolt.

It seems that these elderly gents saw the jousting with the Smithsonian, though quite vicious at times, as a kind of sport. Many of the men appeared to revel in the fight, stirring up their comrades. In the end, it is safe to say the curators and directors and NASM knew they weren't dealing with a group of "those bomber sissies," or even "pretty boy Mustang flyers." These guys were not afraid to turn ugly or hit with a powerful punch. They would not go away until they got results.

In 1992 the Smithsonian's Thunderbolt was moved into the National Air and Space Museum's west gallery on Washington's Mall, due in no small part to the pressure brought on by P-47 vets. The *Jug Letter* stated, "Certainly this is where that old warrior belongs if its job in World War II is any criterion for membership in this fraternity of those qualified to represent our nation in its most prestigious showplace."

But the following year the Thunderbolt was taken apart and rolled back out the doors, the Smithsonian "sticking to its guns" with plans to display a number of important aircraft in the location temporarily occupied by the Jug. Much to the chagrin of the P-47 flyers, the plane was loaned to the Museum of Aviation at Robins Air Force Base, Georgia.

Once the Thunderbolt was gone from the National

The Smithsonian's choice to not make room for its P-47 Thunderbolt in the World War II gallery of their aviation museum facility on the National Mall was the subject of many a Jug pilot's ire for years. Today, the aircraft is finally on display at the National Air and Space Museum's Steven F. Udvar-Hazy Center near Dulles International Airport. *Author's collection*

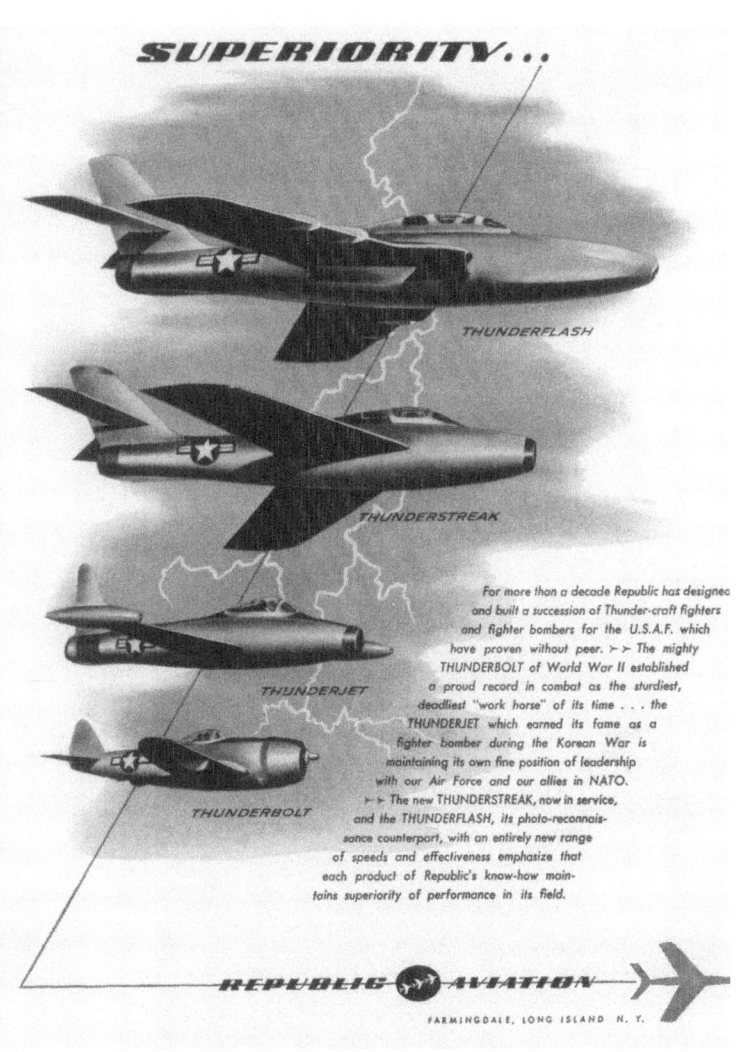

SUPERIORITY...

THUNDERFLASH

THUNDERSTREAK

THUNDERJET

THUNDERBOLT

For more than a decade Republic has designed and built a succession of Thunder-craft fighters and fighter bombers for the U.S.A.F. which have proven without peer. ⊱⊱ The mighty THUNDERBOLT of World War II established a proud record in combat as the sturdiest, deadliest "work horse" of its time . . . the THUNDERJET which earned its fame as a fighter bomber during the Korean War is maintaining its own fine position of leadership with our Air Force and our allies in NATO. ⊱⊱ The new THUNDERSTREAK, now in service, and the THUNDERFLASH, its photo-reconnaissance counterpart, with an entirely new range of speeds and effectiveness emphasize that each product of Republic's know-how maintains superiority of performance in its field.

REPUBLIC AVIATION

FARMINGDALE, LONG ISLAND N.Y.

Many say that the Thunderbolt was Republic's greatest achievement. Years later, the workhorse P-47 is referred to in the company's publications and advertisements. Republic went on to make other notoriously tough fighters, including the many versions of the F-84 Thunderjet and the Vietnam-era F-105 Thunderchief. *The Museum of Flight, Hatfield collection*

Mall, one Jug pilot wrote that he felt he was "sadly at a disadvantage" when he overheard some German visitors admiring the Focke-Wulf Fw-190 on display. He told his fellow airmen, "And I couldn't say to them, 'Yeah, and *this* is the plane that kicked the [expletive deleted] out of it!'" Luckily for everyone involved (except maybe the Germans), the Smithsonian put both the Focke-Wulf Fw-190 and the beloved P-47 Thunderbolt on perma-

nent display in 2003 at the Steven F. Udvar-Hazy Center near Dulles International Airport.

Incidentally, the fight with the P-47 Thunderbolt Pilots Association failed to deter the Smithsonian from asking the group for a $100,000 donation for display, support, and exhibitry for the embattled Jug. The 962 members of the association voted on the proposal and rejected it by eight votes. As one member wrote, "The National Air and Space Museum has a duty to display prominent aircraft. We should not have to pay them to do what they are supposed to do in the first place."

NEW DISCOVERIES

Just when it seems that every existing Thunderbolt is gone, or at least housed in a museum, a new airframe bobs to the surface. In 1993, a Dutch vessel surveying to dredge a new channel in the Zuider Zee hit something underwater at a depth of three meters. They discovered the object was a smashed P-47 fighter of the 4th Fighter Group. When the aircraft was lifted free of the water, searchers discovered the remains of the pilot still in the cockpit. His dog tags solved the mystery; he was Flight Officer Frank Gallion, missing on November 11, 1943, after a fight with German Messerschmitts.

Twelve years later, the Traunsee, a lake in northwest Austria, gave up a Thunderbolt that had been lost on one of the last missions of the European war. The general location of the Thunderbolt at the bottom of the Austrian lake had been known ever since it crashed on May 8, 1945. Four fighters from the 405th Fighter Group were racing toward home at high speed and low level over the lake after a morale-boosting flight over a recently liberated concentration camp at Ebensee. The propeller of *Dottie Mae*, piloted by Lt. Henry Mohr, touched the lake's surface while the plane was zooming along at more than two hundred miles per hour. The big fighter bounced once, shooting a huge cloud of spray in all directions, and then plunged into the water. Nearby boaters rescued the stunned and nearly drowned pilot.

The Traunsee is quite large and very deep—more than six hundred feet in some places. So, though there was no doubt *Dottie Mae* was there, it was going to take time, effort, and money to locate and retrieve the airframe.

After years of searching, the plane was found in 2005. It was lying in 210 feet of water, on its back, partly covered in silt. Once wrestled to the surface, the new owner, Brian Kenney, could finally see what was left of

In 2005, *Dottie Mae* was lifted to the surface of Lake Traunsee, in northwest Austria, after decades under water. The P-47D shows evidence from its high-speed crash into the water at nearly level attitude: crushed lower nose, mangled tail, and missing flaps. *Walter Höllhumer*

the old bird. The bottom was crushed due to the P-47's high-speed collision with the water. The propeller and flaps were torn free, but all in all, the big fighter was remarkably intact. The plane's pin-up girl artwork and name were still clearly visible on the side of the fuselage.

The plane was packed into two large crates for shipping "home" to the United States—one more rare Thunderbolt survivor left in the world.

APPENDIX

Republic P-47B Thunderbolt

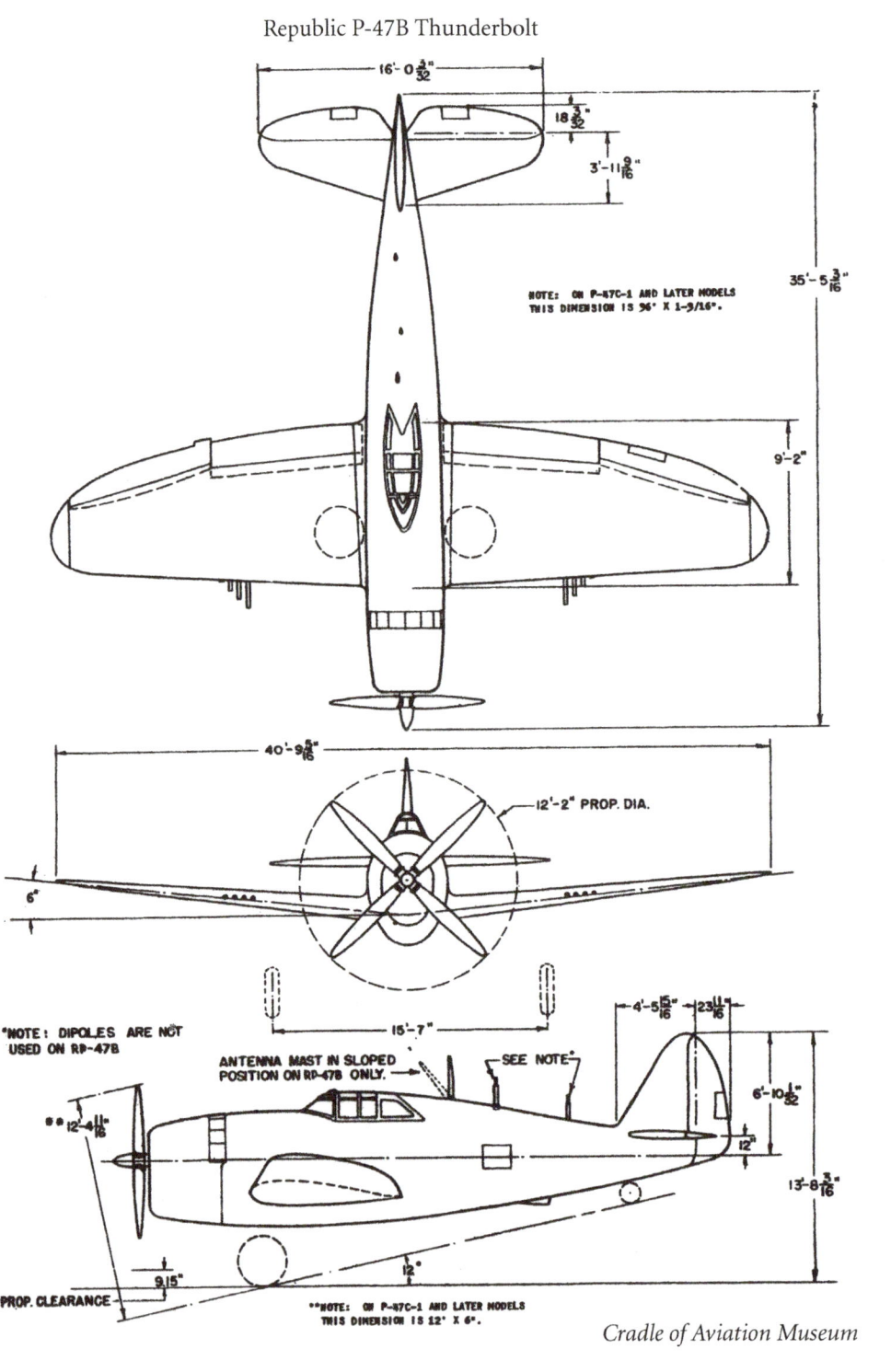

Cradle of Aviation Museum

P-47 OPERATIONAL STATISTICS*

1943 TO AUGUST 1945

Sorties	545,575			
Combat Flying Hours	1,352,810	Aircraft Probably Destroyed, Air		431
Total Flying Hours	1,933,596	Aircraft Probably Destroyed, Ground		147
Gallons of Gasoline Consumed	200,504,000	**Total**		**578**
Tons of Bombs	132,482	Aircraft Damaged, Air		1,313
.50 Caliber	134,899,415	Aircraft Damaged, Ground		2,916
Cannon	755	**Total**		**4,229**
Rockets	59,567			
		Locomotives		9,000
Combat Losses	3,499	Railway Cars		86,000
To Enemy Aircraft	824	Tanks and Armored Vehicles		6,000
To Antiaircraft	1,642	Trucks		68,000
Other	1,033			
		Aerial Box Score		
Non-Combat Losses	1,723	(losses vs confirmed victories)		4.6%
Due Enemy	21	Combat Loss Rate per Sortie, less than		0.7%
Other	1,702	Total Loss Rate per Sortie, less than		1.0%
Total Losses	5,222			
Total Production	15,683			
Claims against Enemy				
Aircraft Destroyed, Air	3,752			
Aircraft Destroyed, Ground	3,315	*According to Republic Aviation Corporation and the		
Total	**7,067**	P-47 Thunderbolt Pilots Association		

SELECTED BIBLIOGRAPHY

Bodie, Warren M. *Republic's P-47 Thunderbolt: from Seversky to Victory*. Hiawassee, GA: Widewing Publications, 1994.

Brulle, Robert V. *Angels Zero: P-47 Close Air Support in Europe*. Washington, DC: Smithsonian Institution Press, 2000.

Colgan, Bill. *World War II Fighter-Bomber Pilot*. Blue Ridge Summit, PA: Tab Books, 1985.

Dean, Francis H. *America's Hundred Thousand: the U.S. Production Fighter Aircraft of World War II*. Atglen, PA: Schiffer Publications, 1997.

Freeman, Roger A. *The Mighty Eighth*. London: Cassell and Co., 2000.

————. *Thunderbolt: a Documentary History of the Republic P-47*. New York: Scribner, 1979.

Hagedorn, Dan. *Republic P-47 Thunderbolt: The Final Chapter*. St.Paul, MN: Phalanx Publishing, 1991.

Hess, William N. *P-47 Thunderbolt en Action*. Paris: Éditions E.P.A., 1982.

————. *P-47 Thunderbolt*, London: Arms and Armour, 1989.

Lambert, John W. *The Pineapple Air Force: Pearl Harbor to Tokyo*. St. Paul, MN: Phalanx Publishing, 1990.

Maloney, Edward T. *Sever the Sky: Evolution of Seversky Aircraft*. Corona del Mar, CA: Planes of Fame, 1979.

McDowell, Ernest R. *Thunderbolt: the Republic P-47 Thunderbolt in the Pacific Theater*. Carrollton, TX: Squadron Signal Publications, 1999.

McDowell, Ernest R. and William N. Hess. *Checkertail Clan*. Fallbrook, CA: Aero Publishers, 1969.

Morgan, Len. *Famous Aircraft: the P-47 Thunderbolt*. Dallas: Morgan, 1963.

P-47 Thunderbolt, the "Jug," The. New York: P-47 Thunderbolt Pilots Association, 1981.

Pilot's Manual for the Republic P-47 Thunderbolt. Milwaukee, WI: Aviation Publications, 1973.

Scutts, Jerry. *P-47 Thunderbolt Aces of the Ninth and Fifteenth Air Forces*. Oxford: Osprey, 1999.

Stanaway, John C. *Kearby's Thunderbolts*. Atglen, PA: Schiffer Publications, 1997.

Stoff, Joshua. *Thunder Factory: an Illustrated History of the Republic Aviation Corporation*. Osceola, WI: Motorbooks International, 1990.

Woerpel, Don. *The 79th Fighter Group over Tunisia, Sicily, and Italy in World War II*. Atglen, PA: Schiffer Publications, 2001.

INDEX

Other books in the At War series:

Battleship Arizona's Marines at War
978-0-7603-2717-3

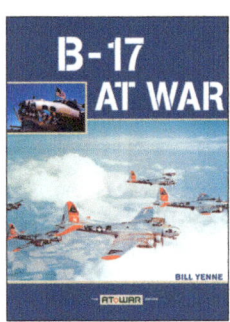

B-17 at War
978-0-7603-2522-3

Iwo Jima Recon
978-0-7603-2993-1

Other Zenith Press titles of interest to the enthusiast:

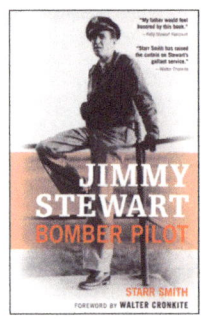

Jimmy Stewart, Bomber Pilot
978-0-7603-2199-7

Shot to Hell
978-0-7603-1609-2

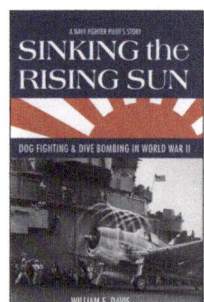

Sinking the Rising Sun
978-0-7603-2946-7

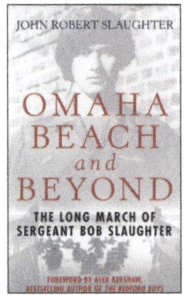

Omaha Beach and Beyond
978-0-7603-3141-5

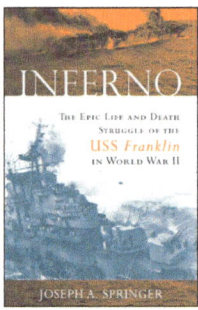

Inferno
978-0-7603-2982-5

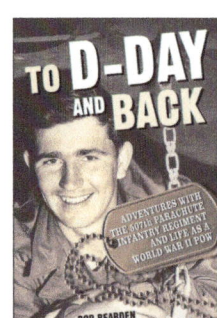

To D-Day and Back
978-0-7603-3258-0

Find us on the internet at www.zenithpress.com 1-800-826-6600

CPSIA information can be obtained at www.ICGtesting.com
Printed in the USA
LVOW01s2300240814

400673LV00004B/4/P